"Associate pastors remind me of someone assigned the middle seat between two overweight men on an airplane—the senior pastor on one side and the congregation on the other. It can be tough to get comfortable and get anything done. Dr. Michael Mauriello has written a thoughtful and well-researched guide for associate pastors who want to understand the dynamics and strategic advantages of their role. He not only understands the position, but he can help pastors serve effectively from the middle seat."

—Lee Eclov,
retired pastor;
adjunct professor, Trinity Evangelical Divinity School;
columnist, PreachingToday.com;
author of four books for pastors

"Dr. Michael Mauriello is a trusted wise guide to associate pastors seeking to understand their complex role in church ministry. Michael's research is fueled by his love for God and the desire to see pastors flourish. *Associate Pastors: Ministry from the Middle* is a must-read for Christian leaders."

—Deborah Colwill, PhD,
associate professor of Educational and Leadership Studies,
Trinity Evangelical Divinity School

"As Michael Mauriello points out, associate pastors must be secure in their own relationship with God and skilled in the art of facilitating ministry from 'the middle.' By thoughtfully synthesizing insights from current resources, the author presents six critical tasks that the associate pastor would be wise to adopt. This is a much-needed contribution to resources addressing the unique role of associate pastors—those who 'navigate complicated relationships as a pastoral practice.'"

—Donald C. Guthrie, EdD,
executive director, Center for Transformational Churches,
Jeanette L. Hsieh Chair of Educational Leadership
and director of the PhD (Educational S̶t̶u̶d̶i̶e̶s̶),
Trinity E̶

Associate Pastors

Ministry from the Middle

Michael Matthew Mauriello

KREGEL
MINISTRY

Associate Pastors: Ministry from the Middle

© 2022 Michael Matthew Mauriello

Published by Kregel Academic, an imprint of Kregel Publications, 2450 Oak Industrial Dr. NE, Grand Rapids, MI 49505-6020.

ISBN 978-0-8254-4744-0

Printed in the United States of America

22 23 24 25 26 / 5 4 3 2 1

*To Londa, Lee Eclov, and to the memory of
Ted and Margaret Ward*

CONTENTS

Figures 9

Tables...11

Acknowledgments 13

Introduction: The Challenges of Being in the Middle...........................15

Chapter 1. Management Is (Part of) Ministry.....................................39

Chapter 2. Relationships in Organizations 67

Chapter 3. Learning in Organizations 81

Chapter 4. Associate Pastors as Facilitators of Learning.....................101

Chapter 5. Pinched Associate Pastors..113

Chapter 6. Learning Wide and Deep Roles 137

Chapter 7. Associate Pastors as Player-Coaches 153

Chapter 8. Six Critical Skills for Ministry in the Middle...................171

Afterword: Preparing Students for Associate Ministry........................209

Bibliography 217

FIGURES

Figure I-1. The Pinched Associate Pastor..35

Figure 2-1. Role Pairs versus Role Sets..69

Figure 2-2. Structuralism and Interactionism..70

Figure 3-1. How Theories-of-Action Are Revised in an
Organization Through Learning...96

Figure 4-1. Associate Pastor and Congregational Learning Loops.......107

Figure 5-1. Senior Pastor and Associate Pastor Relationship..............122

Figure 5-2. Senior Pastor, Board, and Associate Pastor Relationships ...125

Figure 5-3. Senior Pastor, Board, Congregation, and
Associate Pastor Relationships..126

Figure 5-4. Senior Pastor, Board, Congregation, and
Key Leader Relationships...133

Figure 5-5. Other Associate Pastor Congregational Frameworks.........135

Figure 8-1. Associate Pastors with Governing Boards..........................173

Figure 8-2. Other Associate Pastor Congregational Frameworks.........174

Figure 8-3. The Five Negotiating Tables...179

Figure 8-4. Reporting and Accountability versus Stewarding Agency ..184

Figure 8-5. How Associate Pastors Learn and Teach...........................187

Figure 8-6. How Learning Spreads Through Associate Pastors............187

Figure 8-7. Followership and Associate Pastor Experiences.................190

Figure 8-8. Integrating the Six Critical Tasks.......................................195

TABLES

Table 3-1. Variations of Individual and Organizational
    Learning Loops..88

Table 5-1. Participants Describing Associate Pastor Frameworks 134

Table 7-1. Associate Pastor Strategies for Facilitating Learning 164

Table 8-1. Associate Pastor Strategies for Facilitating Learning 185

ACKNOWLEDGMENTS

I would like to thank the team at Kregel for all their help in publishing this book, particularly to Carl Simmons for his amazing help in making the text smoother and more readable. Thanks to Shawn Vander Lugt for his help with editing and layout. Thanks also to Robert Hand for walking me through the publication process and his fantastic help from beginning to end. Thanks to Kevin McKissick for his help with the cover and marketing. Obviously, any mistakes in the book belong to me, and not to them.

I would also like to thank those who encouraged me in this project, including my professors Don Guthrie and Deborah Colwill; my late mentors Ted and Margaret Ward; my friends Elizabeth Bjorling Poest and Lyle Enright, who both particularly encouraged me to keep writing; and for my small group, who prayed for me while I wrote. Thank you to all the associate pastors who agreed to the interviews, who opened up about their experiences, and who trusted me with my questions. Without them, the project would have been impossible.

I would also like to thank Lee Eclov for being a great pastoral mentor. And of course I want to thank my wife Londa and my girls, Lillian and Grace, who allowed me to write and bring this book to completion. I love you all so very much.

INTRODUCTION

The Challenges of Being in the Middle

Pastoral ministry is a complicated, stressful, and relationally taxing vocation; associate ministry is no exception.[1] This book is about and for associate pastors. It examines the nature of their work and how they can steward the stressful complexity and ambiguity of being in the middle of congregational dynamics.

Let this metaphor unpack the stress of the being in the middle: Ever get your finger pinched between a closing door and the doorjamb? You probably weren't expecting it; you just had your finger carelessly resting against the door frame. Maybe the door wasn't swinging shut with a lot of force, but it didn't matter. The pressure of the door closing on the jamb pressed on your finger, and you experienced a sharp, perhaps excruciating pain. For a few days, your finger was very tender—and you were pretty wary of putting your finger anywhere near an open door.

Associate pastors often feel that way. Without realizing it, they are pinched between intense pressures and expectations from different relationships in their churches. The next two personal stories are examples from my own ministry: the first a negative experience, and the second a positive example of being in the middle.

---

1   Esa, "Issues in Ministry Effectiveness for the Associate Pastor," 1; Hawkins, "An Evaluation of Selected Dallas Theological Seminary Alumni of Assistant and Associate Pastor in the Local Church;" Danyluk, "The Process of Hiring Associate Pastoral Staff in Congregationally Governed Churches with a Worship Attendance of under 300," 30; Ngo, Foley, and Loi, "Work Role Stressors and Turnover Intentions."

My first church had just implemented a new child protection policy for students in our children's and youth ministries. The policy required that all volunteers submit to a background check to serve as chaperones and mentors. Much energy, work, and passion had gone into designing, passing, and communicating this policy. Ministry leaders were responsible for enforcing it.

My middle school ministry had just begun a monthly hangout time with sixth graders. This new program was a dream of one set of parents who recruited another mother of a sixth grader in the church. Unfortunately, she had not yet submitted a background check. Just as the first evening was getting under way, the mother entered the church gym, plopped down her purse, and looked expectantly at me.

"Sorry I'm late. What do you want me to do? I've come to help out."

Anxiety and fear coursed through me. "But you haven't gone through our background check."

"What do you mean?" she asked. "I'm a parent. I want to participate."

I was pinched. I was caught between my need to fulfill the requirements of an elder-approved policy that was immutable, the intense desire of a mother to participate in her child's ministry, and my volunteer parents who had recruited this mother who had been in the church for years. I searched for the right words. But my anxiety didn't help me find them.

"I'm sorry. Our church policy says you can't until you've completed a background check," is what I wanted to say. But what came out was just, "You can't."

She looked at me with eyes full of her own anxiety and confused anger. "I thought this was our church," she said passionately as she left.

I had fulfilled the policy, but deeply hurt a member of our congregation.

About a year later, she and I restored the relationship through the shepherding of a caring elder. It took courage on both her part and mine. The story ended well, but it also illustrates a clear point: associate pastors of all stripes—whether children, youth, worship, adult, or outreach—are often caught in the middle of complicated relationships and groups in their congregations. It's a genuine struggle many associate pastors feel. Being in the middle is complicated, organizationally confusing, and emotionally taxing. Yet it also brings with it a form of power that can only be gathered and utilized from being in the middle: the power to steward ambiguity.

Take this second story: In my first youth ministry role, I found it odd that the sixth graders in our church didn't attend our middle school youth group, especially since they attended the town's public middle school. Our church had a robust Wednesday night elementary school program which went through sixth grade, but several sixth-grade students along with their parents wanted to participate in middle school ministry. The elementary program director and I talked about moving sixth graders to the middle school ministry several times, but we couldn't come to an agreement about where the group belonged.

An elder met with me and the elementary program director to resolve the question. I planned my presentation to ask that sixth graders be moved to the middle school ministry. I didn't think my proposal would be accepted. I was caught between two other leaders in an ambiguous situation. So, I created a third option: the church could treat the sixth grade as a transitional year. One week a month the sixth graders would participate in the middle school ministry; the rest of the month they would participate in their regular ministry. At the meeting the elder and the program director passed on my first idea, but they both agreed to the other option! I had been pinched in the middle, but had stewarded the ambiguity by proposing a new course of action that worked for everyone involved.

Where Did the Idea for This Book Come From?

As you might guess, this book was born out of my experiences as an associate pastor. This short life history explains where my passion for this topic came from.

While studying architecture at college, I experienced a clear call to pastoral ministry. After college I went immediately to an evangelical seminary just north of Chicago. On the second day of class my ministry professor warned the class, "Seminary does a great job of preparing you for your last ministry position, but it doesn't necessarily prepare you for your first two or three positions. Let me encourage you to take education and leadership classes that will help you in roles like youth ministry, worship, or other associate ministry roles."

Wanting to do well when I graduated, I took his advice and took several classes in youth ministry and Christian education. I did my field education at a local church in the youth group, children's ministry, and outreach ministry. I thought I wanted to be a "lifer," a pastor who spends his or her entire life working in youth ministry, so I took a role as a youth pastor at an evangelical church in rural Illinois after graduation.

That first pastorate lasted five years to the day. While I started out in youth ministry, soon I was also in charge of a summer young adult program. Eventually I had an adult Sunday school class. I left that congregation to embark on a new journey to earn a PhD, unsure of what the future would hold. Shortly thereafter, I received a second call to the church where I served while in seminary. I was there for almost six years and had broad responsibilities including children, youth, adult, outreach, and pastoral counseling ministries.

I had fruitful ministry in both churches, developed amazing friendships, learned, and grew in my relationship with Jesus. I am deeply thankful that the Lord directed me to both places. I am particularly grateful to my senior pastor at my second church, Lee Eclov, who mentored me and risked having a PhD student as a full-time associate minister. It was here that I could see a new vision for my life as a teacher of ministry students.

That said, ambiguity was a regular experience in both of my churches. There were challenges in relating to senior pastors as superiors and friends, and to my volunteers as *their* superior and friend. I had ambiguous relationships with my elder boards as a non-elder in my first church and as a nonvoting elder in my second. I felt ill-equipped to handle these relational issues when seminary ended; I had to quickly develop new skills in managing resources, developing teams, and coaching volunteers. I felt squeezed between different constituencies within the churches: volunteers, parents, elders, youth, and staff. I was often confused about when to ask leaders to follow specific instructions and when to let them "do their own thing." While much of my ministry in both churches was fruitful, I often doubted my overall effectiveness. I particularly struggled with casting vision in ways that both honored my senior pastors and respected my volunteers.

Many of my associate pastor colleagues described similar tensions in their ministries. Some had comparable experiences; others had far more difficult pastorates. Some considered abandoning ministry but chose to stick out the stress and painful relationships; others left ministry for other careers. I wanted to discover how associate pastors move in complicated and ambiguous relationships in order to have fruitful pastorates. So, after researching what others had written about associate ministry, I interviewed twenty-five associates to listen to and understand their experiences. The result is this book.

Who Are Associate Pastors, and What Do We Know About Them?

When I write for and about associate pastors, who do I mean? An associate pastor is any clergy in a local congregation who does not occupy the senior pastoral role in a church. The following description captures associate ministry well: "All pastors must be servants, but the associate pastor, by the nature of the position, is charged with serving, supporting, and equipping God's people and to do so under the direction of the senior pastor."[2] According to this definition, youth pastors or worship pastors are associate pastors, even though they only oversee one specific area of ministry. However, associate pastors are also sometimes generalists with a wide array of responsibilities, and not just specialists in a specific niche ministry such as children, youth, young adults, worship, or other focused ministry.[3] In my first church, I was a specialized youth pastor. In my second pastoral role, I was a

---

2   Rudnick, *The Work of the Associate Pastor*, 2–3.
3   Johnson, "Preparing an Associate Pastor to Become a Senior Pastor"; Haskins, "An Examination of the Role and Function of the Associate Pastor in the United Methodist Church"; Radcliffe, *Effective Ministry as an Associate Pastor*; Rudnick, *The Work of the Associate Pastor*.

generalist over children, youth, young adult, adult, small group, and some outreach ministries. But in both my roles I directly reported to and had direct contact with my senior pastor.

While associate pastors have wildly differing roles and responsibilities, research on associate pastors describe three common elements to associate ministries. First, associate pastors depend on having constructive relationships with their senior pastors. Second, associate pastors are the managers of their congregations. Third, associate pastors have ambiguous roles.

Relationships with Senior Pastors

Senior pastors are certainly critical partners for associate pastors. While associates are under the direction of the senior pastor,[4] who they support,[5] assist,[6] and who prescribes their duties,[7] there is often substantial overlap in those duties[8] which might also create ambiguity. The term "collaborator" is sometimes used to refer to the associate.[9] Associate pastors are often encouraged to be supportive of their senior pastors either through upward management,[10] through noncompetitive relationships,[11] and/or through exercising compatible gifts.[12]

Associate Pastors as Managers

As you might expect, there is more to the associate's role than the relationship to the senior pastor. While management clearly intersects with being in a subordinate position to a senior pastor, associate pastors are often referred to as "second chair leaders" in their

---

4   Rudnick, *The Work of the Associate Pastor,* 2–3.
5   Rudnick, *The Work of the Associate Pastor;* Hawkins, "An Evaluation of Selected Dallas Theological Seminary Alumni of Assistant and Associate Pastor in the Local Church."
6   Hawkins and Sallman, *The Associate Pastor,* 17.
7   Radcliffe, *Effective Ministry as an Associate Pastor,* 144.
8   Sam, "The Formation, Mentoring, and Socialization of the Associate Pastor into the Pastorate in the Roman Catholic Church"; Overman, "Associate Pastor as Collaborator."
9   Esa, "Issues in Ministry Effectiveness for the Associate Pastor," 171; Overman, "Associate Pastor as Collaborator," 11–12; Rudnick, *The Work of the Associate Pastor,* 95.
10   Smith, "Playing Second Fiddle on One String: The Role of the Associate Pastor," 92.
11   Rudnick, *The Work of the Associate Pastor.*
12   Esa, "Issues in Ministry Effectiveness for the Associate Pastor," 62–64.

organizations.[13] Bonem and Patterson coined this term and describe a second chair leader as someone "in a subordinate role whose influence with others adds value throughout the organization."[14] Second chair leaders provide relief for senior pastors in terms of implementing a church's specific vision: "They are managers of the process towards a realized vision."[15]

"Management" can sound rather alien to the pastoral identity and imagination. What does it mean to be a manager? Management has classically been understood as a linear or cyclical process of planning, organizing, coordinating, and controlling.[16]

If this definition sounds a little bit like the floor manager in a factory, or a middle manager in an organization, that is exactly what is being described. In fact, one researcher suggests that associate pastors share critical tasks and are essentially identical to mid-level managers in mainstream workplaces in their practice of leader-manager practices.[17] Other authors describe associate pastors as those who create, implement, and manage "specific functions" of a congregation;[18] support the vision, mission, and staff of a church;[19] or plan, organize, staff, direct, and control as managers.[20]

But most seminarians or Bible school students don't imagine pastoral work as managerial. They want to preach, teach, disciple, care

---

13   Gilbreath, "An Administrative Manual for the Associate Pastor"; Haskins, "An Examination of the Role and Function of the Associate Pastor in the United Methodist Church"; Woodruff, "Executive Pastor's Perception of Leadership and Management Competencies Needed for Local Church Administration"; Griffin, "Vision Building as a Second Chair Leader for a Large Congregation"; Akinde, "A Study Comparing the Leadership and Management Characteristics of Associate Church Pastors and Mid-Level Corporate Managers and Leaders."

14   Bonem and Patterson, *Leading from the Second Chair*, 3; emphasis original.

15   Griffin, "Vision Building as a Second Chair Leader for a Large Congregation."

16   Mintzberg, "The Manager's Job," 49; cf. Mackenzie, "The Management Process in 3D;" Kraut, et al., "The Role of the Manager," 123–24.

17   Akinde, "A Study Comparing the Leadership and Management Characteristics of Associate Church Pastors and Mid-Level Corporate Managers and Leaders."

18   Hawkins, "An Evaluation of Selected Dallas Theological Seminary Alumni of Assistant and Associate Pastor in the Local Church," 10; Hawkins and Sallman, *The Associate Pastor*, 17.

19   Rudnick, *The Work of the Associate Pastor*, 2–3.

20   Radcliffe, *Effective Ministry as an Associate Pastor*, 144.

for other people, or actively evangelize nonbelievers. Management is often not taught in theological education.

When you work in a factory, management is guided by a common goal of creating the product the factory and its staff were hired to create. But a church does not create a product, because it is not a factory, nor is it a business. The church is a miracle community of the new humanity redeemed by Jesus Christ. But congregations are nonetheless organizations, networks of intentionally structured relationships working toward a common goal or vision.

Congregations ought to have a theological and biblical vision for contextualizing ministry. However, associate pastors, like senior pastors, are often caught in a culture of ambiguity.

Ambiguity and Associate Pastors

What do we mean by ambiguity?

Have you ever been sent on an errand to the grocery store to buy a specific brand of tomato sauce, but that tomato sauce was sold out? Your phone is dead, so you cannot call anyone to get advice or direction. You face the shelves and see a myriad of options: different brand names, different prices, different flavors, different ingredients for customers with different allergies or food sensitivities. What do you pick? If you are at all like me, this scenario can produce anxiety because there is no way to get more information about which jar to pick. I am forced to choose, and that choice requires me to navigate ambiguity—a lack of information, direction, or structure that impedes action or decision-making.

Here is a more relevant example to ministry. As a newly hired associate pastor, I was reviewing files when I discovered a volunteer who was already serving but had not completed a required application and background check (the previous pastor had forgotten the paperwork). I called the volunteer to explain, and asked him to complete the forms. He was irritated, since the previous pastor had given him permission to serve. The volunteer was caught in ambiguity; he had the previous pastor's support but didn't have the technical clearance from the church. I too was caught in ambiguity; I didn't know that

the volunteer had been incorrectly onboarded, and now I was unsure what to do to rectify the situation without hurting feelings or
disrupting the ministry.

Ambiguity is obviously a form of stress. In fact, stress and ambiguity go hand in hand, and they can benefit or plague any number of
people in any number of roles. Stress is generally defined as a person's
perception that the demands of their environment are greater than
their ability and resources to meet that need.[21] Stress is a dynamic state
of uncertainty[22] coming from or concerning a person's specific role,
organizational sources, or relationships.[23] Environmental situations
within organizations put extraordinary pressure on an individual.[24]
Two major sources of stress in organizations are role conflict and role
ambiguity.[25] Role conflict occurs when expectations of the role do not
match reality.[26] Various kinds of role conflict include:

- Experiencing different expectations from one person
- Experiencing different expectations from different people
- Experiencing different expectations arising from membership
  in multiple organizations
- Experiencing a moral conflict based on roles
- Experiencing role overload: expectations exceed the holder's
  ability to perform within a limited time[27]

Role ambiguity is a particularly powerful, though not always
negative, form of organizational stress.[28] Role ambiguity can be de-

---

21 Stout and Posner, "Stress, Role Ambiguity, and Role Conflict," 747; Cooper, et al.,
    Organizational Stress, 27.
22 Stout and Posner, "Stress, Role Ambiguity, and Role Conflict," 747.
23 Cooper, et al., *Organizational Stress*, 1, 27.
24 Stout and Posner, "Stress, Role Ambiguity, and Role Conflict," 747.
25 Kahn, et al., *Organizational Stress*; Rizzo, House, and Lirtzman, "Role Conflict and
    Ambiguity in Complex Organizations"; Van Sell, Brief, and Schuler, "Role Conflict
    and Role Ambiguity"; Faucett, Corwyn, and Poling, "Clergy Role Stress."
26 Van Sell, Brief, and Schuler, "Role Conflict and Role Ambiguity," 44.
27 Kahn, et al., *Organizational Stress*, 20; Van Sell, Brief, and Schuler, "Role Conflict and
    Role Ambiguity," 44.
28 Kemery, "Clergy Role Stress and Satisfaction."

scribed as a lack of required information necessary for an incumbent to know how to perform his or her role.[29] It can also be defined in terms of predictability of outcomes due to behavior and the existence of environmental guides for behavior.[30] Role ambiguity can also relate to available information about the expectations associated with a role, methods for fulfilling known role expectations, and the consequences for role performance.[31]

Role ambiguity is often tied to task conflict, or conflict about how tasks are performed in the opinions of different stakeholders, as well as relational stress such as tension, animosity, and annoyance. Therefore, role ambiguity and task conflict are often emotionally charged. Further, role ambiguity can have a negative relationship to self-efficacy, since it reduces available information on which to evaluate performance and visualize performance.[32]

Let's attempt to illustrate role ambiguity with the following story that describes role task conflict. One of my churches initiated a summer New Testament reading program composed of two elements: an individual reading plan to be completed at home and weekly gatherings where participants would discuss the week's reading. The program consultant emphasized the need for *both* the individual reading and the weekly gathering. My senior pastor felt that the weekly meetings were unnecessary and did not want to require them. As the program implementor, I was caught between different expectations placed upon me by the senior pastor and the consultant. Both gentlemen were polite yet assertive in their positions. After some debate, we proceeded by holding weekly meetings but not requiring attendance.

Here is another illustration that describes role ambiguity, this time through lack of information. Our church was fortunate to have a military band leader as a member. My senior pastor thought it would be a wonderful outreach to our neighborhood to ask one of

---

29   Kahn, et al., *Organizational Stress*, 73.
30   Rizzo, House, and Lirtzman, "Role Conflict and Ambiguity in Complex Organizations," 156.
31   Van Sell, Brief, and Schuler, "Role Conflict and Role Ambiguity," 44.
32   Li and Bagger, "Role Ambiguity and Self-Efficacy," 368.

the bands stationed at the local military base to perform a church concert, and he gave me the responsibility of putting the concert together and advertising it in the surrounding area. I had never done this kind of task so I had to learn quickly and through trial and error where to gather resources, where to advertise, what to set up, and what people to recruit. The nature of the task was ambiguous and produced stress. In the end the concert was successful, and I had gained new skills in promoting events, but it took some time to shake off the anxiety.

To review, ambiguity is the presence of stress from numerous sources that inhibits identifying or resolving problems, usually combined with anxiety in the form of relational pressure or the lack of resources to discover or enact solutions to a problem. In other words, ambiguity implies the stress that accompanies unknown situations or conflicting expectations, with the accompanying pressure to resolve the unknown in an effective or fruitful manner.

The Uneasy Relationship Between Pastoral Ministry and Management

It is no wonder then that associate pastors often struggle to make sense of their roles. Theological schools from Bible college to seminary do not emphasize management in their curriculum. In addition, pastors are often suspicious of leadership, as well as of management practices and literature in the church, compounding the problem of poor management.[33] Pastoral theologian Thomas Oden suggests that seminarians often reject administrative studies toward ministry as crass, manipulative, and corruptive; and he concedes that "business leadership techniques" are sometimes uncritically adopted into congregations.[34] Branson and Martínez, without denying the importance of leadership, describe modernity's influence on leadership in the church, and push back on command-and-control styles of strategic

---

33 Radcliffe, *The Effective Ministry of an Associate Pastor*, 26–28; Boersma, "Managerial Competencies for Church Administration as Perceived by Seminary Faculties, Church Lay Leaders, and Ministers," 2.

34 Oden, *Pastoral Theology*, 154.

planning, consumerism, and "the church's self-understanding as a volunteer organization."[35] Guder voices a similar set of concerns:

> At the denominational, local, and seminary levels, the management paradigm dominates models of leadership development as if it were a neutral set of techniques and skills. The nature of leadership is thus transformed into the management of an organization shaped to meet the spiritual needs of consumers and maximize market penetration for numerical growth.[36]

Particularly, there is suspicion of the church growth movement and "McDonaldization."[37] McDonaldization is a form of management that promotes a more bureaucratic and hierarchical approach to organizations.[38] McDonaldization emphasizes efficiency, calculability, predictability, and control—and results in a dehumanizing rationalism as well as anonymous or impersonal relationships.[39] Watson and Scalen suggest that churches are "restructuring themselves according to a corporate business model."[40] Smith and Pattison go so far as to write,

> Western Christianity's symbiotic relationship with industrialization had led to attempts to circumvent the messy or inefficient facets of faith. Many churches, particularly those driven by church growth models, come dangerously close to reducing Christianity to a commodity that can be packaged, marketed, and sold.[41]

---

35   Branson and Martínez, *Churches, Cultures, and Leadership,* 210–11.
36   Guder, *Missional Church,* 198.
37   Smith and Pattison, *Slow Church*; Watson and Scalen, "Dining with the Devil"; Drane, *The McDonaldization of the Church.*
38   Ritzer, *The McDonaldization of Society*; Drane, *The McDonaldization of the Church.*
39   Ritzer, *The McDonaldization of Society,* 13–14.
40   Watson and Scalen, "Dining with the Devil," 17.
41   Smith and Pattison, *Slow Church,* 14.

Drane summarizes many pastors' fears when he writes, "An over-emphasis on what is quantifiable will generally hinder if not undermine personal and spiritual growth."[42] Willimon, while stating that a manager is a good image of the pastor, echoes this concern and suggests that pastoral management cannot be measured purely by efficiency or productivity, especially when unexpected events or concerns occur to occupy the pastor's time and attention.[43]

Yet Oden also states, "Experienced clergy . . . know all too well that they must function effectively as leaders in the church and community and be responsible for complex organizational processes."[44] Nonetheless, while most pastors enter the ministry to pursue preaching, teaching, and discipleship, they are often surprised by the tasks of leadership and management for which seminary did not prepare them.[45]

The Shift in Management Paradigms

There has been a shift in how management is perceived by scholars and practitioners. With the emergence of learning organizations, managers have developed a new role described as a facilitator of learning[46] who functions much like a coach in their organization.[47] Such a leader is tasked with helping others achieve their goals by programming learning to enhance creativity.[48] Facilitative leadership is a large shift from a command-and-control understanding of management to an understanding of manager as a people developer,[49] which may require

---

42 Drane, *The McDonaldization of the Church*, 47.
43 Willimon, *Pastor*, 61–62.
44 Oden, *Pastoral Theology*, 154.
45 Burns, Chapman, and Guthrie, *Resilient Ministry*, 199–200.
46 Ellinger, Watkins, and Bostrom, "Managers as Facilitators of Learning in Learning Organizations"; Ellinger and Bostrom, "An Examination of Managers' Beliefs about Their Roles and Facilitators of Learning."
47 Ellinger and Bostrom, "Managerial Coaching Behaviors in Learning Organizations"; Ellinger, "Antecedents and Consequences of Coaching Behavior"; Hargrove, *Masterful Coaching*, 2008.
48 Guastello, "Facilitative Style, Individual Innovation, and Emergent Leadership in Problem Solving Groups," 226–77.
49 Ellinger, Watkins, and Bostrom, "Managers as Facilitators of Learning in Learning Organizations," 106.

a shift in identity,[50] as well as a shift in belief and mental models to lean into that identity.[51] Facilitative leadership is the opposite of impositional (or command-and-control) leadership,[52] and could be described as "helping people in groups transform themselves, their community, and their world."[53] This new paradigm reflects that direction and knowledge are not locked at the top of an organization; they are spread throughout all of the constituents.

While management is indeed unavoidable, it should not be seen as the ugly stepsister of ministry responsibility. A shift to a facilitator of learning or facilitative leadership seems to fit pastoral responsibilities, especially when one considers the pastoral responsibilities of teaching and preaching against the backdrop of Ephesians 4.

The Benefits of Stewarding Ambiguity

So far in this chapter, I've stated that associate pastors are pinched in the middle of critical agents and constituents in their churches as significant managers of their congregations, even if that is not how they prefer to understand their role. This pinched middleness with its managerial emphasis comes with intense stress, often in the form of role ambiguity.

That said, Kemery[54] notes that in pastoral ministry, role ambiguity is not always a bad thing. In fact, when role ambiguity is high but role conflict is low, pastors tend to report a high level of job satisfaction because they have the ability to make decisions in order to act on the ambiguity they experience.[55]

It is simply a given that organizations experience ambiguity in the face of making decisions and accomplishing goals. Forester states that decision-makers face incomplete information about problems

---

50 Ellinger and Bostrom, "An Examination of Managers' Beliefs about Their Roles as Facilitators of Learning," 159.
51 Ellinger and Bostrom, "An Examination of Managers' Beliefs about Their Roles as Facilitators of Learning," 148.
52 Fryer, "Facilitative Leadership," 26.
53 Hargrove, *Masterful Coaching*, 15.
54 Kemery, "Clergy Role Stress and Satisfaction," 566.
55 Kemery, "Clergy Role Stress and Satisfaction," 566.

and their backgrounds, alternatives and their potential consequences, and the range of values and preferences among stakeholders—all in the context of limited time, skills, and resources.[56] This requires managers to assist in sensemaking in their organization,[57] but it also requires them to lead organizations to steward the ambiguity so that possibilities for moving forward emerge through organizational discernment.[58] In short, if managers can navigate the complexities of their organizations from their inherent middleness,[59] they may become stewards of ambiguity through the process of facilitating learning in their organizations.

This opportunity, then, is what makes the associate pastoral role significant and unique. Associate pastors can make a big difference by acting as stewards of ambiguity, particularly if they can take on the identity of a facilitator of learning within their congregations.

Good News for Associate Pastors!

This paradigm ought to be good news for associate pastors, especially those associate pastors who serve in congregations large enough to have significant complexity but small enough where associate pastors have regular ongoing contact with all levels of the organization. This new paradigm made me wonder if associate pastors, while perhaps being unaware of the role of facilitator of learning, functioned as such in their congregations—and if they did, how they went about it.

I researched how associate pastors functioned as facilitators of learning in their congregations. In order to discover this, I attempted to answer three important questions:

1. How do associate pastors navigate complexity in their congregations?
2. How do associate pastors facilitate their own learning?

---

56 Forester, *Planning in the Face of Power*, 50.
57 Weick, *Sensemaking in Organizations*.
58 Barton, *Pursuing God's Will Together*; cf. Scharmer, *Theory U*, 7–8, 60.
59 Oshry, *In the Middle*, 80.

3. How do associate pastors facilitate the learning of other con-
    gregational members?

How Was the Research Conducted?

Before moving on, it is important to share how I conducted
the research presented in this book. I knew I was asking significant
research questions about associate ministry, so I wanted to be able
to capture the experiences, perceptions, and language that associate
pastors use to describe themselves. I relied on participants sharing
their stories, thoughts, and experiences, in order to gather data that
could be organized into themes. This research methodology, called
qualitative research, usually engages in forms of interviews, focus
groups, and site visits to gather data. While the participants provide
the data, the researcher is the "instrument" of discovery.[60] While I
used an interview protocol to guide the conversations I had with
associates, I interjected questions in real time and used the protocol
as a guide to answer my research questions.

As you read, I'll introduce you to twenty-five different associate
pastors who perform a variety of different tasks for their churches. They
come from a wide variety of Protestant denominations including the
Evangelical Free Church of America, Evangelical Anglican Church,
United Methodist Church, Presbyterian Church USA, Nazarene
Church, Assemblies of God, different Baptist churches, and nonde-
nominational churches. Nine of the participants were women, three
were African American, and two were Asian American. Most of these
associate pastors work in suburban areas, but four serve in an urban
context, and four minister in a rural or small-town setting. I found
these participants through a snowball method: I interacted with people
who knew associate pastors or were themselves associate pastors and
asked them to suggest participants who would be able to provide rich
experiences, and therefore helpful data, for the study. By following this
approach, I was able to meet and interview many Caucasian males, but
it was much harder to find women and minorities to interact with in the

---

60   Merriam and Tisdell, *Qualitative Research*.

study. I found most of these minority participants either by cold-calling or through networking with friends in different denominations.

In deciding who to interview, I looked for associate pastors who met three common attributes. First, all of them ministered in churches that were larger than one hundred regular attenders but were smaller than 1,750 regular attenders. Why is church size important? A mega-church is described as having membership or regular attendance of two thousand worshippers or more. Megachurches can have dozens of associate pastors or staff, and I am sure that they also experience a middleness of a kind. But there is an important difference with pastors and staff in megachurches: they are not in a position to have access to all the levels of organization. Put another way, associate pastors in megachurches cannot see the top and bottom of their congregations the way associates in smaller churches can. The associate pastors interviewed could all see the top and bottom; they were familiar with all the ministries and layers of responsibility of their churches. This type of access also brought a reciprocal benefit: everyone in the church had some level of access to the associate pastors.

Second, all the associate pastors had at least five years of pastoral ministry experience. Why be concerned about time? Five years or more of tenure provides associate pastors with enough time to be able to commit to professional reflection. Five years of elder board meetings, staff meetings, volunteer interactions, teaching, constructing, or buying curriculum. Five years of good, mediocre, or bad events that have shaped their pastoral identity and practice.

Third, all of them were in a reporting relationship to a senior or executive pastor; if they reported to an executive pastor, the associate pastor also had consistent recurring contact with the senior pastor. This may seem an obvious requirement, but as we have already seen, the senior pastor relationship is a potent partnership. There are many churches that are not megachurch-sized which now employ executive pastors, but associate pastors still have formative relationships with their senior pastors in these relationships. I'll show you how the executive pastor relationship impacts the associate pastor role as we discuss our findings.

In addition, all the associate pastors had two of the following three attributes: 1) they had completed at least one theological degree in a seminary, Bible college, or liberal arts school; 2) they had received ordination in their denomination, or had an equivalent ministerial endorsement from their congregation; 3) they had five years of pastoral experience in addition to the minimum five years listed above, giving them at least ten years of experience with congregations.

Why do these criteria matter? These three attributes describe significant steps on the path to forging the pastoral identity of a minister, not only in their own minds but also in the minds of their congregations or larger denominations. These three criteria also ensured that enough training, effort, or time had gone by that the associate pastor could reflect biblically and theologically on his or her own ministerial experience.

I gathered the data for the study in two stages. For the first stage, I interviewed each of the associate pastors in their church offices and spoke with them for about an hour, recording the conversations and taking notes as our interviews went along. Afterward, I transcribed and examined the interviews for themes, and then organized the themes into different categories. When I met with the associate pastors, I went through an interview protocol that allowed me to interject new and different questions based on the answers of their pastors:

1. Tell me about your church and how you serve your congregation.
2. Which people do you interact with most in the congregation? What is it like to work with them?
3. How do you partner with key people in the congregation to do ministry?
4. What does being an associate pastor look like in your congregation?
5. How do you develop yourself professionally as an associate pastor?
6. How has your professional development assisted you in your pastoral role?

7. How intentionally does your congregation determine learning goals for itself?
8. How intentionally do you determine learning goals for your ministry?
9. What learning is occurring in your congregation?
10. How are you able to nurture learning in your congregation?

For the second stage, I invited seven of the participants back for focus groups. Four participants were in the first focus group; three were in the second. In this stage, I presented my preliminary findings and asked the groups to offer feedback on my categories. As before, I recorded these meetings, transcribed them, and coded them for themes, revising my initial categories. I had no interview protocol for the focus groups; I simply presented the data and started a free-flowing conversation.

What to Expect as You Continue to Read

Allow me to give a little roadmap to the remainder of the book. Chapter 1 will provide a biblical and theological argument that situates management as a genuine element of Christian ministry empowered by the Holy Spirit. With this foundation in place, chapters 2 and 3 will set the stage for describing associate pastors as facilitators of learning. Chapter 2 will describe how roles and complexity emerge in organizations; chapter 3 will review how learning occurs in organizations and apply that knowledge to the facilitator-of-learning role. Chapter 4 will integrate organizational theory with theology to make the case that associate pastors are facilitators of learning.

In chapters 5 through 7, I will describe the themes that came out of the interviews with the twenty-five associate pastors I interviewed. Chapter 5 will answer the question, "How do associate pastors navigate the complexity in their congregations?" Chapter 6 will answer the question, "How do associate pastors facilitate their own learning?" And chapter 7 will answer, "How do associate pastors facilitate the learning of others in their congregation?" In these chapters I will use the stories and words associate pastors share about their ministry positions, the tasks they perform, and the relationships they encountered there.

In chapter 8, I will describe the implications of that research and will argue that the most important skill an associate pastor can possess for facilitating learning and managing ambiguity is relational competency. The Afterword will suggest how theological education can better equip associates for their roles.

Summary of the Study

Now remember, the associate pastors who participated in the study came from churches that were of more than one hundred regular participants and less than 1,750; they can see the top, the middle, and the bottom of the organization. The findings can be summarized by one essential word: "pinched." What does that "pinchedness" look like? The following diagram was composed from the themes and findings from my interviews with the twenty-five associate pastors. While other authors have already written about the roles associate pastors have with other organizational stakeholders,[61] this study describes how associate pastors see the interconnections in their congregational relationships. These interconnections are visualized in Figure I-1 below.

Notice some important features of this figure. First, associate pastors saw themselves as clearly at the center of all of the relationships in their churches. Second, while associate pastors have one-on-one relationships with the other participants described in the chart, these relationships are not purely linear; the constituents are networked in a web of relationships. The relationship with key volunteers, as we will see, turned out to be just as challenging and formative to the associate pastor's role as that of the senior pastor. Third, the associate pastors are triangled, or "pinched," between different groups. This set of relationships presents both challenges and opportunities for associate pastors in their unique roles.

---

61   Radcliffe, *The Effective Ministry of an Associate Pastor.*

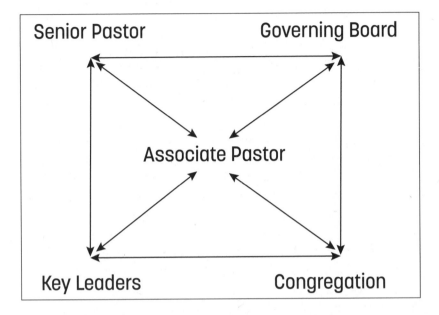

Figure I-1: The Pinched Associate Pastor

It is important to keep in mind that these diagrams are not organizational charts, but rather a description of how associate pastors perceive that they relate to other constituents in their churches. They demonstrate that describing associate pastor relationships as purely linear command-and-control relationships does not account for the complexity of how an associate pastor experiences the day-to-day relationships of his or her congregation.

The diagram presented above is not the only way associate pastors described their congregations. Depending on the church's governing structure, associate pastors could find themselves in a differing set of pinched relationships, depending on the polity of the church (cf. Figure 5-5 or 7-2).

What were the implications of the study? If associate pastors are inherently in the middle of their congregations, what is it imperative that they know and understand about their congregations? Here are the five major takeaways that I will discuss in subsequent chapters:

1. *Navigating Anxious Relational Triangles:* Psychologist Michael Bowen described anxiety as the crucial emotion that human beings experience and must take into account when interacting with others in their families, communities, and organizations. Much has already been written about the Bowen triangle; I will take that research and apply it to this study in chapters 2 and 8.

2. *Negotiating Political Interests:* Many new pastors are shocked to discover that congregations are political communities, with different constituents attempting to act on their concerns and interests. Yet associate pastors need not be afraid of political organizations; humans are political beings and church members can engage in sanctified politics to the glory of God. Associate pastors play a crucial role in the political activities of their congregations; they must learn to negotiate their interests and the interests of others in a godly way.

3. *Stewarding Agency:* The task of ministry does not fall to pastors alone, but to the entire congregation. Associate pastors realize the power and gifting that those above and below them have to accomplish the work of their congregations. Associate pastors must therefore be prepared to help others succeed by stewarding the agency of all the congregational participants in their churches.

4. *Directing Learning:* Associate pastors are often the educational workhorses of their churches who organize their own learning and the learning of the entire congregation, often attempting to align it with the goals or mission of the congregation. Associate pastors direct knowledge throughout the organization and train others to do the work of ministry, while keeping leaders aligned to followers.

5. *Practicing Followership:* As noted previously, the associate pastor's relationship with the senior pastor is very important. Followership is the study and practice of following leaders well. Associate pastors sometimes face particularly challenging problems in followership that they must mitigate from the middle.

Management is clearly as pastoral a practice as preaching, administering the Lord's Supper or baptism, providing pastoral counsel, or visiting the sick, among others. Yet in many pastors' minds, it's the ugly stepsister of those other pastoral practices. Associate pastors must rescue this practice in their own minds and step into the role of managing. Shepherding, a biblical metaphor for pastoring, provides a superb image for managing and the pastoral task.

In suggesting these implications, I want to be clear then that managing in a congregation is not primarily about preparing budgets, tracking calendars, publishing newsletters or bulletins or reports, posting social media items, or ordering curriculum and other supplies. I am suggesting that managing in a congregation is primarily about shepherding relationships in a Christ-honoring manner so that ministry moves through the entire congregational structure. My central claim is that the most important skill associate pastors require is the ability to navigate complicated relationships and to understand the navigation of these relationships as a pastoral practice. By mastering the ability to navigate complicated relationships, associate pastors can become stewards of ambiguity in their congregations.

Some Thoughts for Other Readers

While I am primarily writing for associate pastors, it is my hope that senior pastors might read this book—especially if they are thinking of hiring their church's first associate pastor, if they have never had an associate pastor of any kind report to them before, or if they are finding themselves struggling to understand the tensions faced by their associate pastoral staff. If you are a senior pastor, let me please say a few words to you.

I understand that ministry and staff relationships for senior pastors are complicated as well. While my research didn't examine how senior pastors experience middleness, I am sure that you experience a kind of pinching all your own, though I think it is a safe assumption to think that the form of middleness you experience may take on different dimensions and have different implications than it does for the associates you currently or will oversee on your pastoral staff.

Nonetheless, I hope that this book casts light on some of the pressures and tensions that associate pastors face. Please pay attention to the various relational dynamics that associate pastors have with their senior pastors, and the complicated relationships they have with other constituents that make their ministries troubling or energizing. By knowing these things, I hope it will become more possible for you to facilitate the agency of your own staff.

It is also my hope that theological educators in seminaries and other Christian higher education organizations will read this book. If you are a ministry professor or trainer, I hope you will see that the pivotal skill of navigating complex relationships is underdeveloped in many future associate pastors by the time they graduate from theological education. I know that seminary cannot possibly train and equip a future pastor for every necessary skill, but I think back to what my professor said on the first day of class in seminary: "You need to be prepared for your first job." Surely there is a better way of helping associate pastors master this skill than leaving it to "on-the-job-training." It is my hope that this book provides a critical glimpse into the heart of associate ministry and that it gives you some grist for thinking through the curriculum of the seminary. I will offer some suggestions in the Afterword.

If you are an unpaid or paid ministry director—whether part-time, full-time, or part-time bivocational associate pastor, I hope you will read this book too. I think you will find many of the descriptions and implications are transferable to your situation, even if you've never been to seminary or haven't gone through the process of being ordained.

Lastly, if you are in seminary, earning a theological degree, or preparing for ministry, I hope you will read this book as well. It is my hope that this book will expose you to the blessings and challenges of being an associate pastor, and that it will help you channel your passion for biblical and theological knowledge in the direction such knowledge is always meant to travel: toward loving God by loving his people well.

CHAPTER 1

Management Is (Part of) Ministry

Any human action taken in the world depends on his or her understanding of what the universe is and why it exists. As Alasdair MacIntyre says: "I can only answer the question, 'What am I to do?' if I can answer the prior question, 'Of what story do I find myself a part?'"[1] In other words, all human action is related to an understanding of the universe. It's no less true when it comes to the why and how of associate pastors managing ministry than it is for a baker making apple pie. In fact, Christian ministry in all of its facets is deeply dependent on the metanarrative of Scripture.[2]

This chapter seeks to create a biblical and theological case for management to be a part of Christian ministry. I'll lay out my argument by examining critiques of the picture and place of ministry in the church by theologians, explore a theology of human calling as it relates to management generally, and build a theology for management as a part of pastoral ministry.

Historical Paradigms for Ministry

The Introduction made the case that there is some distrust of management literature and theory among some pastors. This first

---

1   MacIntyre, *After Virtue*, 216.
2   Bartholomew and Goheen, *The Drama of Scripture*, 19–21.

section elaborates on that distrust while continuing to advocate for management as a pastoral task.

Recent missional scholarship has examined how church leaders were imagined from the apostolic period through early Christendom to modernity.[3] Guder suggests that these changes reflect a change starting with Christendom where the church, operating from societal margins in a missional orientation toward the world during the apostolic and early church age, moved to the center of culture after Constantine's conversion. In the early church, leadership was apostolic; that is, it reflected the sent nature of the church as an emissary and witness to Jesus Christ. After Constantine's conversion, leadership was envisioned as a priesthood that was separated through a complicated hierarchy from the typical Christian laity.[4]

The Reformation reimagined the church leader as pedagogue: "The Reformation challenged and reformed the inherited priestly categories of leadership only to create a more pedagogical identity for the clergy in which such leaders became the keepers and guarantors of the Word."[5] The Enlightenment, with its epistemological shift focusing on rationalism and scientific discovery rather than revelation, pushed the church to conceive of the pastor as a professional on par with doctors or lawyers.[6] Professional ministry is conceived as a set of discrete tasks to be performed by pastors which require training in higher education and seminary.[7]

> The three revisionist images of counselor, manager, and technician illustrate that the churches appropriated without question modern images of the leader as their primary means of equipping their leadership for a return to the cultural center.[8]

---

3   Guder, *Missional Church*, 190.
4   Guder, *Missional Church*, 190.
5   Guder, *Missional Church*, 193.
6   Guder, *Missional Church*, 194–95.
7   Guder, *Missional Church*, 195.
8   Guder, *Missional Church*, 196.

Guder is particularly critical of modernity and secular humanism's managerial influence on church leadership. Goheen and Bartholomew describe humanism as secular, naturalistic, rational, and scientific.[9] Building off Aquinas's distinction between the sacred and secular,[10] secularism suggests that the created world (nature) functions autonomously from God's work.[11] As the sacred becomes further challenged in the wake of the Enlightenment, humans attempt total mastery over nature by rational and scientific means,[12] including the sphere of social sciences.[13] God becomes more and more unnecessary to achieving an ideal human future.[14] The story of the universe is that humans sit in the place of a nonexistent or distant God, and they may choose to operate in the universe in autonomy.[15]

Recognizing organizational literature's indebtedness to modern humanism (particularly scientific technique and rationality), Guder points out that modern management is not merely a set of skills but is ethically loaded: "They are rooted in presuppositions about how the world is constructed and about human control of that world." He is particularly concerned about the concept of effectiveness which assumes that the control of processes yields desirable ends, but that these ends are "defined in terms of market, consumption, and privatized personal need."[16] Guder argues that any form of ordained hierarchical leadership stands against the priesthood of all believers, and prevents the church from repossessing a missional orientation from the margins of society.[17]

Van Gelder takes a similar stance. Describing the medieval and Protestant church as the established church, he suggests that the

---

9   Goheen and Bartholomew, *Living at the Crossroads*, 69.
10 Goheen and Bartholomew, *Living at the Crossroads*, 79.
11 Goheen and Bartholomew, *Living at the Crossroads*, 84.
12 Goheen and Bartholomew, *Living at the Crossroads*, 84.
13 Goheen and Bartholomew, *Living at the Crossroads*, 98.
14 Goheen and Bartholomew, *Living at the Crossroads*, 96.
15 Goheen and Bartholomew, *Living at the Crossroads*, 92–93.
16 Guder, *Missional Church*, 197.
17 Guder, *Missional Church*, 195.

church in the Enlightenment took on an orientation that he names the "corporate church." Recognizing their development in North American contexts, he uses the term "corporate church" to describe churches that are voluntary and democratic in nature[18] and organized around a purposeful intention.[19]

McKnight's assessment of ecclesiology in church history is that Christendom and the Protestant churches offered an attractional approach to church versus a missional or incarnational orientation. While he cites Guder's paradigm, he is not opposed to priestly, pedagogical, or professional themes of ministry as long as they are squarely situated in a missional paradigm of ministry.[20]

Guder is correct in terms of paradigm, but is open to question in terms of practice. Certainly pastors are not professionals in the sense that they are merely masters of techniques; ministry can never be reduced to management as a scientific and rational discipline pursuing human autonomy. This approach is functionally secular and thus devoid of the Spirit's power. Van Gelder is likewise correct that the church ought not be reduced to a corporate paradigm where churches function as autonomous voluntary organizations versus a divinely appointed, gathered, and sent people.[21]

Nonetheless, any gathered group does organize; and as will be seen below, both God and the apostles impose organization on the church in Scripture, including specifically selected and endorsed leadership and guiding mission and worship for the congregations they birth. Further, some of these individuals provided explicit guidance in managing—that is, directing resources and people. Churches have organization both in their human relationships and in the tasks and practices that orient their communal life and mission. Therefore, ministry and management, while not equivalent, are connected in the grace of the Lord Jesus Christ.

---

18   Van Gelder, *The Ministry of the Missional Church*, 76.
19   Van Gelder, *The Ministry of the Missional Church*, 75.
20   McKnight, *A Community Called Atonement*, 77.
21   Van Gelder, *The Ministry of the Missional Church*, 84–86.

Management as Spiritual Practice

Lest we think theologians are alone in considering the spiritual dimensions of management, Drucker defines management as a culturally embedded practice moving toward a common end or goal emanating from common purposes and values; it is primarily about people, their learning, and their development.[22] Therefore, he suggests that management is actually a liberal art, *as well as a spiritual practice*, since it involves understanding the nature of humanity as well as good and evil.[23] Covey also writes about the spiritual dimension of management, describing it as "your core, your center, your commitment to your value system"[24]; and Greenleaf writes about the influence of good and evil on individual and corporate action, as well as ethics, healing, and love.[25]

While management is a spiritual practice, not all management theorists write from a Christian perspective. Current organizational theorists such Senge and colleagues are deeply indebted to non-Christian religious traditions in their theoretical moorings.[26] Bohm and Bateson, who influence these authors, are themselves indebted to Eastern traditions.[27] Since these scholars are influential in the marketplace, explicitly non-Christian theological worldviews are influencing practice. Theology and spirituality already have influenced management. Consequently, management is a theological Christian practice and important to the pastoral task. "Management is not just a necessary evil, as some would perhaps view it, but a ministry given by God. Therefore, the application of [biblical] principles in Christian organizations is not only morally correct but also biblically proper."[28]

---

22 Drucker with Maciariello, *Management*, 20–21.
23 Drucker with Maciariello, *Management*, 24–25.
24 Covey, *7 Habits of Highly Effective People*, 292.
25 Greenleaf, *Servant Leadership*, 28, 29, 39, 49, 52.
26 Senge, et al., *Presence*, 12; Nonaka, "A Dynamic Theory of Organizational Knowledge Creation," 29–30; and Hawkins, "The Spiritual Dimension of the Learning Organisation," 176–77.
27 Bohm, *Wholeness and the Implicate Order*, 25; *On Dialogue*, 47, 80; Bateson, *Steps to an Ecology of Mind*; cf. Hawkins, "The Spiritual Dimension of the Learning Organisation," 177.
28 Boersma, "Managerial Competencies for Church Administration as Perceived by Seminary Faculties, Church Lay Leaders, and Ministers," 24.

A Short Review of Human Vocation

Again, I want to be clear that I am not advocating that the dominant theme of human calling is management any more than I am advocating that the dominant ministry of the church is management. Neither is true; human flourishing is not equivalent to good managing. The highest pursuit of human calling is to know and love the God who is the Father, Son, and Holy Spirit forever by participating in the triune life through the Son (Deut. 6:3; John 17:3). Management does not claim pride of place in common human experience any more than education, family, art, agriculture, government, economics, or production. Yet I am emphatically claiming that management is part of humanity's calling and Christian ministry, and that as such it is good and worthy of theological reflection for human flourishing as both part of creation and of our redemption in Christ.

Short Narrative Theology: Creation and Fall

The biblical story situates human creation and God's purpose in ordering light and life in the context of darkness and chaos. All of God's actions in creation are good, and all lead to the creation of space, time, and conditions for plant, animal, and human life to flourish (Gen. 1:1–31). God appoints lights to rule day and night (1:14–19), and on earth he appoints human beings to rule and take dominion over the created order (1:28). At the same time God blesses both human (1:28) and animal life (1:22) as he provides for them to multiply and fill the earth.

Just as sun, moon, and stars are enmeshed in the heavens that they order and rule (Gen. 1:14–19; cf. Ps. 8, Ps. 19), so humans depend on the created order (1:29) and are systemically embedded in it (Gen. 1:24–26; 2:7). Yet humans are still privileged as God's image in creation (1:27). God needs no idol and wants no image (Exod. 20:3–4), since humanity is his image. Since the purpose of an image in the ancient world was to declare the presence of power of a deity in a geographic place,[29] God's reign and rule are declared in the humans

---

29   Walton, *Ancient and Near Eastern Thought and the Old Testament*, 117–18.

he desires to fill with himself (Eph. 1:10, 23; 3:19; 4:5). God's Spirit is meant to animate Adam and draw him into the life of triune God (Gen. 2:7; cf. John 20:21–22).

Human work in creation is modeled on priestly activity.[30] Consider that Genesis 1 conceives of the universe as God's cosmic temple; and consider that Adam and Eve's work in the garden is "working" and "keeping" the ground. While immediately applicable to horticulture, these two words are also words that describe the priestly work of the tabernacle.[31] The garden's structure is a high place,[32] and Adam and Eve are kingly priests tending a paradise that belongs to God that he shares with humans. Heaven and earth touch in Eden. That God also blesses for the task and provides both covenant promises and boundaries highlights the priestly function of Adam and Eve's gardening (Gen. 1:22–24, 28–30; 2:15–16). Human work is thus always embedded worship, enmeshed in the conditions of the world that God has placed humans in and from which they were taken.

Human rebellion assaults God's order but it does not utterly undo it. When Adam and Eve transgress God's appointed boundary (2:17; 3:6–7), they make a choice between life and death (2:17; 3:2–3)—a decision that also foreshadows Israel's choice between keeping God's covenant or rejecting it (Deut. 30:15–20; cf. Josh. 24:14–15). By stepping away from covenant relationship with the living God, Adam and Eve submit themselves to death as sin becomes their master (cf. Gen. 4:7; Rom. 6:12, 16). Thus their calling is made much harder as they hide (Gen. 3:8–10), alienate (3:12–13), and oppress (3:16). Their removal from Eden demonstrates a break in their life with God (3:22–23), but not in God's work in their lives as he covers their shame (3:21) and provides them with children (3:21; 4:1, 25). God remains committed to the life of his creation and his human imagers.

---

30 Wright, *The Mission of God's People*; Walton, *The Lost World of Genesis One*.

31 Cf. Num. 3:7–8; Waltke with Fredricks, *Genesis*, 87, 101; Wenham, *Genesis 1–15*, 67; Wright, *The Mission of God's People*, 51–52.

32 Divinely protected trees, presence of life-giving water, angelic beings, and God's own divine presence; cf. Walton *Ancient Near Eastern Thought and the Old Testament*, 124–25.

So God's commission "to work and to keep" is passed on to Adam's descendants and retains its priestly dimension. Abel keeps sheep while Cain tills the ground, both of which they offer in sacrifice (4:2–3). Noah also keeps animals on the ark (6:20–21) and plants a vineyard (9:20). Like a good priest, Noah sacrifices (8:20) and blesses (10:26–27). The commission to fill (9:1, 7) and rule (9:2) is in fact renewed as God blesses Noah's family and makes a covenant with them, the animals, and all creation (9:8–17). This covenant reemphasizes the human roles as embedded creational stewards and imagers (9:6), as well as God's commitment to humanity in blessing and providing provision for their calling (9:3–4). Even after the flood, God remains committed to the life of his creation and his human imagers.

Yet the commission is bent. Cain's offering is rejected because he does not do what is right (4:5); sin is now vying to be his master versus the God who made him (4:7). Cain rejects Abel as bone of his bone, preferring to control creation and worship on his own terms as he asks, "am I my brother's keeper?" (4:9). Noah becomes drunk on his fruit and exposes his nakedness (9:20), echoing Adam and Eve's story of eating and nakedness (3:7).

So bentness remains after the flood. The people of Shinar twist technical innovation (baked bricks) and industrial cooperation to create a name for themselves rather than submit to God's rule (11:1–4). Foreshadowing Israel's slavery to build cities and bake bricks in Egypt (Exod. 1:11; 5:8–18), human vocation takes an idolatrous turn that God personally and intentionally opposes and overthrows (Gen. 11:5–9; cf. Exod. 3:19–22). At Babel, the people, like Adam and Eve in the garden, seek to reign in place of the God they represent.

Abraham and Israel

God continues to remain committed to human life in his election of a nomadic shepherd named Abraham. While the tower builders are unsuccessful at making a great name, God promises one to Abraham, who will be a blessing to all the world and will become a great people with innumerable descendants (Gen. 12:1–3; 15:5). Yet Abram is impotent to make this plan come about because his wife is barren

(11:30) and because he is landless (12:7). Thus, God must move in Abraham to make him fruitful. Abraham learns to depend on God's work and timing as he trusts God's promise (15:6). Abraham takes on priestly dimensions in his dependence in his sacrificing (12:7–8; 13:8; 15:7–10; 22:1–20) and intercession (18:22–33; 20:17). Abraham in his calling is a blessing to all peoples (12:7) as he demonstrates following God's covenant (18:19; cf. 26:5). As such, Abraham becomes paradigmatic of who Israel is meant to be.

Abraham's descendants are also impotent to bring about God's plan. When oppressed as slaves under threat of genocide (Exod. 1:22), God sends another shepherd, Moses (3:1), to bring Israel out of Egypt (3:7–9). Only God can rescue Israel, which he does in the context of the provision of a meal and salvation; new life for Israel comes in the slaying of the lamb at Passover (12:1–28) and is sustained by manna in the wilderness (16:4). God's calling of Israel is not based on their own righteousness (Deut. 9:4–5) or power (7:7; 8:17), but simply on his love for them and for Abraham, Isaac, and Jacob (7:8).

Provision accompanies calling. Israel will be a kingdom of priests and a holy nation (Exod. 19:4–6); and God blesses Israel for this task (Num. 6:24–27; Deut. 33). Like Abraham, their calling does not terminate in themselves. They will show the remainder of the world what humanity under the reign of God looks like. They agree to a covenant relationship with God (Exod. 24), which can be summarized as loving God completely and loving their neighbors as well (Deut. 6:4–5; Lev. 19:17; cf. Mark 12:28–34).

Israel perpetually stumbles in their calling in the wilderness (Num. 14:20–23) and in the land.[33] Yet in spite of this God sends them leaders empowered by his Spirit,[34] flawed though they and the people might be. Though they rejected God as king (1 Sam. 7), God in his grace gives Israel yet another shepherd, David (16:11), who is at once a paradigmatic good king (13:14; 1 Kings 9:4–6) empowered by the

---

33 Cf. Younger, et al., *Judges, Ruth*, on the cycle of idolatry in Judges.
34 Cf. Othniel (Judg. 3:10), Gideon (6:4), Jephthah (11:29), Samson (14:6, 19; 15:14), and Saul (1 Sam. 11:6).

Spirit (1 Sam. 16:13), and yet utterly flawed like Israel (2 Sam. 11, 24). In spite of Israel's impotence, God commits to Israel's commission and empowers them with his very presence. God promises to David a house that God himself will establish, and a Son who will build a temple for Israel (2 Sam. 7).

As the narrative proceeds, Israel perpetually embraces idolatry, choosing death and exile (2 Kings 17:7–20) by embracing injustice (Isa. 59:1–15). The people, like their kings, fail to love God and to love their neighbors with justice. But God refuses to abandon his sinful and impotent people; he promises to be the shepherd who will rescue Israel from a second captivity as their shepherd and from their inability to submit to God's reign (Ezek. 34) by giving them the Spirit (Joel 2:28–29; Ezek. 36:26–29). Just like God's covenant with Noah, this new covenant has cosmic dimensions, since it is coupled to God's commitment to all life in his creation (Jer. 31:35–37; Isa. 66:1–17; Ezek. 34:25–31).

Jesus Christ

Jesus comes as that Good Shepherd who lays down his life for the sheep (John 10:11), as the Lamb of God who takes away sins (1:29, 36). Jesus is sent to give eternal life (3:16; 4:14; 5:21), his very life on the cross so that the Father's very life can come into his people through the Holy Spirit (3:6; 4:23–24; 6:63). Jesus describes this gift as God's provision of life-giving food (6:33). Indeed Jesus says, "my flesh is true food, and my blood is true drink" (6:55) for the life of the world (6:32). Christ transforms both the manna of the wilderness (6:32) and Passover (Mark 14:22), to reflect his crucifixion as the true exodus by which all who believe are gathered back from slavery to sin and death. As the Good Shepherd who gives his life, Jesus's work is profoundly priestly. Jesus declares that he himself is God's temple (John 2:18–19); John the Baptist declares that Jesus is the Lamb of God (John 1:29, 36). Jesus is the great high priest who makes atonement and gives new life (Heb. 4:14–16). This covenant made in his body is marked by the commandment for believers to love one another, this love being a witness to the world of the reality of Christ's reign (John 13:34–35).

The Good Shepherd is also David's true son (Matt. 1:1; 20:30; 21:9; 22:41–45), who will reign over Israel and all nations. But Jesus demonstrates in his ministry to Israel what a good king is like; he is concerned with justice, preserving life, and serving the weak (12:15–21; cf. Isa. 42:1–3) as a servant (Matt. 18:1–4; Luke 22:27). In fact, Jesus reminds his disciples that the anointed Messiah is a servant all the way to death on a cross, and his followers must do the same (Matt. 16:24–28). The way to sharing life is in giving life away, and by joining Christ in his death so we can participate in his life (Rom. 8:16–17; cf. Gal. 2:20; Eph. 2:4–7). As a servant-king, Jesus demonstrates that the way of ruling is the way of loving, reconciling, and servanthood (John 13:1–35).

In doing so, Christ establishes a new humanity (Eph. 2:15; cf. Col. 1:21) from believing Israel and believing Gentiles (Gal. 3:27; Col. 3:11), who when joined to his death and resurrection (Eph. 2:1–10) make up God's temple (2:11–21). This new humanity, the church, is gathered to Christ and then sent into the world, taking on Israel's commission under the lordship of Jesus Christ (1 Peter 2:9). Jesus's death and resurrection inaugurate the eschatological age of the Spirit; the church lives under the reign of Christ now (Matt. 28:18; Rom. 8; Col. 1:15–20; Heb. 2:8–9) in the power of the Spirit, but awaits his return for the fullness of redemption. But the church is to live for the fullness of that reign now, longing for the temple of God's gathered people to be completed (Eph. 2:19–21), and hoping for creation's renewal and rebirth as we witness to the reign of Christ as we await the return of the Good King (Titus 2:13–14). But Jesus does not leave church to navigate the end of the current age on its own; he sends his Spirit to indwell the church and give it life, in the age of sin and death. The Spirit gives life now, ensuring that nothing separates the church from God's love, and empowering her to continue God's work in the world (Rom. 8:2,12–13).

The Narrative's Implications for Management

Human vocation is marked by its creaturely and created dimension. Humans are created by God to work in a relational system of living creatures to rule, but ruling takes the path of serving, since the reign of God is seen clearly in Jesus Christ. Management then is about the stewardship of life and relationships, particularly human relationships from a posture of servanthood. But this life comes from God himself; it is his life in his creation. While managers don't normally farm and herd, all are priests who facilitate the flourishing of life in creation. They bless by equipping and providing others with what is needed to do their work as they discern where God is equipping and providing, in order that God's life may come into the world through the ministry of Jesus in his church.

Management is intensely relational and covenantal work; it cannot be accomplished without God working in a redeemed and diverse human community within the boundaries of committed relationships. The fall bends management to deny inherent human relationality in favor of exploitable or disposable persons (Gen. 4:7). Managers can attempt to replace God in themselves by seizing power in hoarding control. Yet such power grabs are in the end impotent, because they steer managers away from human purpose and cut them off from God's very gift of himself. But in redemption, managers repent and come under the rule of the perfect image, Jesus Christ, who is firstborn over creation and the new creation; and is head of all things for the church.

Managers may follow God's pattern by advancing human flourishing as they participate in the reign of God in Christ in a diverse humanity. They rely on God's power distributed by the Holy Spirit in all of God's people. Management is impotent to bring about human flourishing on its own without God's empowerment and without participation and partnership across the church. Management depends on God's provision as it follows the pattern of God's reign. Management serves in relationships motivated by God's love.

Having situated management in a narrative of human vocation, we can now move to exploring management in the church's ministry under God and through her God-appointed leadership.

The Church, Her Ministry, and the Ministry of Management

The church is not a corporation structured like a business. The church is first and foremost a miracle people that comes about through the incarnation, work, life, death, resurrection, and ascension of the Lord Jesus Christ (Eph. 2:14–18). This people form a communion with God through the mutual indwelling of Christ and our indwelling of him and the Father (John 17:20–24); we share God's very life and love (John 17:1–3).[35] The church is joined to Christ through the work of the Holy Spirit (Eph. 1:13–15) and participates in the divine nature (2 Peter 1:4) as Christ's body (1 Cor. 12:12–14; Eph. 4:4; Col. 1:18), which is also his temple (Eph. 2:21). The church is also a creation of the Holy Spirit, who through the work of Christ regenerates believers (John 3:3–8; Rom. 8:2, 9–10) in order that they may become children of God through faith in Christ (John 1:12; cf. Rom. 8:14–17). The members of the church are indeed truly children of God (1 John 3:1). As such, following the pattern of Israel in the Old Testament,[36] the church is a miracle people made up of believing persons from all ethnicities, Jewish and Gentile (Rom. 1:16–17; Gal. 2:15–17; Eph. 2:11–13), and social standings who God is binding together in Christ to becomes a new humanity and part of God's household (Gal. 3:26–27; Eph. 2:19; Titus 1:7) as sons and daughters of the Father and the bride of Christ (Eph 5:32; Rev. 22:17). The church is also a new kingdom of priests and a holy nation (1 Peter 2:4–10; Rev. 5:9–10; cf. Exod. 19:1–6). Since the church is the community of those God has called and gathered to himself (Eph. 1:11, 1 Tim. 4:10), the new humanity understands that it can do nothing apart from Christ and the Spirit of God (John 15:1–3, 16; 1 Cor. 2:4, 13; 12:4). The church is the triune God's creation (Eph. 2:10).

The Church as Divine and Human Reality

Yet the church is not only a divine reality; it is also a human one. Indeed, human leaders and servants are given by God to the church in

---

35 Seamands, *Ministry in the Image of God,* 12; Reeves, *Delighting in the Trinity,* 80.
36 Cf. Gen. 15, 17, and 18 regarding the miraculous birth of Abraham's son Isaac; Gen. 21:1–6; 25:21–22; 30:22 for God's relief of barrenness to Sarah, Rebekah, and Rachel; Gen. 50:19 for God's deliverance of Jacob's family from famine; Exod. 12:26–27 for Israel's deliverance from Egypt at Passover; and Deut. 7:7; 9:4–5 for God's love of a small and unrighteous people.

the Spirit's equipping and power (1 Cor. 12:7–11; Eph. 4:4, 12–15). Just as the composition of Scripture was a divine and human task (2 Tim. 3:16; 2 Peter 2:20–21), so the work of the church is a divine and human task. God uses human beings and human processes within the church to draw the fullness of his people to himself. Yet this work is only possible through the ministry of the Holy Spirit, whom Jesus gives to his disciples in order to fulfill his mission and ministry (John 20:22; Luke 24:48; Acts 1:4–5; 2:1–4).

Yet, what about the church's structure? If the church is a divine and human endeavor—the Spirit binding human beings together in a new humanity—is it appropriate or right to describe the church in organizational terms? Howard Snyder writes, "At its most basic level the church is a community, not a hierarchy, an organism, not an organization."[37] Yet he also accepts that the church is an institution "in the broadest sociological sense," but only in a "secondary," "derivative," and "functional" sense.[38]

It is certainly true that the church has an organic structure described with organic language such as "body" (1 Cor. 12:1–13; Eph. 4:12–16) and "household" (John 14:1–3; 1 Tim. 3:14–15). Nonetheless, even organic processes have intentional structure and organization. In order to have biological children, a man and woman must each give half of their genetic structure through sexual union to create a new person and grow the family. Families have a relational structure of adult parents and relatives providing care, guidance, boundaries, and opportunities to children. Bodies develop according to regular genetic patterns; when these patterns are interrupted or disrupted, problems arise. Farmers, who are responsible for growing and stewarding organic resources, know that animals need to eat at regular rhythms, need to be kept warm during winter and cool in summer, and need regular medical care. They know they need to water and fertilize crops at regular intervals, know the time of year for planting and harvesting and ploughing, and a host of other or-

---

37   Snyder, *Community of the King*, 73.
38   Snyder, *Community of the King*, 82.

ganizational concerns that impact how the organic life is brought to fruitful maturity.

The church finds its expression in local contextual gatherings of Christians. Paul writes explicitly to the church in particular places (e.g., "To the church that is in Corinth" in 1 Corinthians 1:2, or "to the churches in Galatia" in Galatians 1:2). These local bodies find themselves in need of leadership and instructional guidance about doctrine and practice; as well as instruction about how to organize their internal life and leadership. Indeed, Paul's letters often link the countering of a false teaching (e.g., Gal. 1:6–9) with appointing or clarifying leadership and its dynamics (e.g., 1 Cor. 1:10–14; Titus 1:5) or clarifying order and structure in worship (1 Cor. 12–14). Indeed, Paul notes that without helpful organization led by the Spirit, churches will organize under bad leadership (Acts 20:28–30). John faces similar dilemmas and gives instructions about who may be received into fellowship as a leader and brother (3 John 5) and about what should be done with those who reject authority (3 John 9–10).

Consequently, local bodies of believers naturally organize and need organization in order to come to maturity in both the character and tasks God requires of his people. As Van Gelder says, "The church is. The church does what it is. The church organizes what it does."[39] Marshall and Payne describe the need for organization as architecture over which the organic life of the congregation flows.[40] Indeed, Seamands, following Schwarz, argues that the Bible uses both organic and structural metaphors to describe the church's nature and work:

> In fact, there are points where "the two aspects are so closely intertwined in a single statement that the resulting picture—judged by the standards of linear logic—seems contradictory." As examples, Schwarz cites phrases such as "living stones" (1 Peter 2:4–8) and "growing into a temple" (Ephesians 2:19–22), the description of the Corinthians

---

39   Van Gelder, *The Ministry of the Missional Church*, 17.
40   Marshall and Payne, *The Trellis and the Vine*, Location 59.

as "God's field and God's building" (1 Corinthians 3:9) and the body of Christ as both growing and being built up (Ephesians 4:12, 16).[41]

My argument here is not to establish a preferred church-governing, liturgical, or organizational structure. My point is that congregations of local believers naturally network and do work with one another. In other words, they organize and structure their work. While the church is not a business or a corporation, it is a network of relationships serving a common purpose, which the triune God empowers and gives life to in order that God's work of giving life to the world continues through the witness and ministry of the church. Indeed, Christ himself actually imposes order on the church's relationships and work such that disorder does not detract from her mission and ministry (Eph. 4:11–16). Therefore, the question is not whether congregations are organizations, but rather: How do churches organize themselves and structure their work in accord with the wisdom and guidance of the Holy Spirit?

The Work of God as the Work of the Church

When Jesus is persecuted by the Pharisees for healing a paralyzed man on the Sabbath, he makes a profound argument: "My Father is working until now, and I am working" (John 5:17). Jesus claims that his work is actually a partnership with the Father that reveals who the Father is to Israel. Jesus does nothing by himself, but only "what he sees the Father doing" (5:19). In fact, the Father shows Jesus this work precisely because the Father loves the Son (5:20).

What is the nature of this work? It is giving life to the world. "For as the Father raises the dead and gives them life, so also the Son gives life to whom he will" (5:21). In fact, the Son is sent by the Father to give eternal life to those who believe (3:16). The Son is given for the life of the world (6:51).

---

41   Seamands, *Ministry in the Image of God*, 109; cf. Schwarz, *Paradigm Shift in the Church*, 7.

But this work is meant also for those who believe and receive eternal life from Jesus. "Truly, truly, I say to you, whoever believes in me will do the works that I do, and greater works than these he will do, because I am going to the Father" (14:12). And this makes sense: if the begotten Son of God acts as a pattern for those who are born of the Spirit as children of God, then naturally these children also do the Father's work. And as the Father sent the Son in the power of the Holy Spirit (1:33–34), so believers are sent by the Son in the power of the Holy Spirit (20:22).

Shepherding as God's Work and the Church's Work

Ezekiel provides a powerful metaphor for what God's life-giving work in the church looks like. God takes Israel's leaders, described as shepherds, to task for plundering the flock of Israel (Ezek. 34:1–2). These false shepherds have failed at several critical tasks: they have not strengthened the weak, healed the injured, brought back strays, nor sought the lost (34:4). As a result, the sheep are scattered (34:5–6). Further, these shepherds have fattened themselves on the sheep by eating them and plundering their wool (34:2–3).

Thus, God, in his ministry to Israel, promises that he will search for, find, and gather the sheep from the lands where they have been scattered (34:12); provide food for them in their homelands (34:13–14); and give them rest (34:15). God himself will be their shepherd (34:15), but he will still appoint a human shepherd to rule the sheep (34:23–24).

Jesus directly fulfills this in his healing and teaching ministry in Israel as he proclaims the nearness of the kingdom of God. He has compassion on Israel because they are "harassed and helpless, like sheep without a shepherd" (Matt. 9:36). Such work is at once a proclamation of the need to repent and the communication of God's justice and mercy. For example, Jesus's authority in healing the paralyzed man is closely connected to his authority to forgive sins (Matt. 9:1–8). Jesus's calling of sinners is at once a rebuke of Israel's leaders but also a declaration of divine mercy (Matt. 9:10–13; cf. Hos. 6:6).

Finally, Jesus's ministry of healing is connected with his lordship over the Sabbath, and again at once a rebuke of Israel's leaders, a declaration of God's justice, and an invitation to enter God's rest (Matt. 12:9–14). Jesus, in partnership with the Father's work, acts as Israel's Good Shepherd (John 10) and declares that his ministry reveals who the Father is in his work of giving rest (Matt. 11:25–29). But he also appoints his disciples to continue his ministry alongside him, giving them authority to do all he has done (Matt. 10:1, 7). This continues after the resurrection, where Jesus appoints Peter to feed his sheep as a shepherd (John 21:15–19). Peter passes this commission on to the church leaders he addresses in his letters (1 Peter 5:1–4).

How the Church Shepherds: The Structure of the Church's Ministry

Again, pastoral ministry cannot be simplified to the administrative tasks of local congregations. If the ministry of the church is to be simplified to one word, that word would be "witness." Just as the apostles were witnesses to the resurrection (Luke 24:48; cf. 1 John 1:1–3), so they were to be Christ's witnesses to Jerusalem, Judea, Samaria, and the ends of the earth (Acts 1:8) in the power of the Holy Spirit (John 20:22; Acts 1:4–5, 8). Yet the witness of the church is multifaceted, which requires pastoral ministry to be multifaceted. If Acts 2:42–47 is a guide for the gathered ministry of the church, then proclamation and prophecy, discipleship or teaching, fellowship, service, and communal worship are five critical tasks of pastoral ministry.[42] If Jesus's ministry is a guide for the church's dispersed ministry in the world, it would include healing as an act of mercy and justice, preaching, and teaching. "These activities—preaching, teaching, and healing—are also the vocation of Jesus's disciples."[43]

Yet, management is clearly necessary for this work in both the church's gathered and sent modes. Oden describes management and

---

42   Parrett and Kang, *Teaching the Faith, Forming the Faithful*, 134–35; Pazmiño, *Foundational Issues in Christian Education*, 45–49; Dean, *Practicing Passion*, 153–54.
43   Guder, *Missional Church*, 133; cf. Matt. 10:1, 5–8

administration as stewardship; he states that pastors steward both the ministry of the gospel and the resources of the church:

> Although all Christians are in a sense stewards, pastors are called to stewardship of a special sort, as "stewards of the mystery of the gospel" (*"oikonomous mustēriōn theou";* 1 Cor 4:1) to whom the sublime mystery of God's self-disclosure have been entrusted. The pastor is also the steward of the resources of the community and charged with the administration of the work and mission of the church. When Paul tries to compare this responsibility with other forms of human responsibility, he finally concludes that is incommensurable (vv. 2–5). No human court can quite grasp this responsibility. It can only be judged by God eschatologically."[44]

The Plurality of Ministry

If God ministers to humanity in creation and in recreation as a shepherd, then God is the first minister.[45] But God is three persons in one nature; Christians worship the Father, the Son, and the Holy Spirit. While united by a single nature, the three persons are distinct from one another, and have union with one another as they participate in ministry together. The eternal begottenness of the Son and the eternal procession of the Spirit from the Father and the Son are mirrored in their work in creation and salvation. The Father speaks through the Son as his eternal Word at creation (Gen. 1; John 1; Col. 1:15; Heb. 1:1–2) and the Son's Word of creation is sustained by the presence of the Spirit (Ps. 104:2–30). The Father sends the Son to give eternal life to all who believe (John 3:16), and the Spirit empowers his mission (1:32–33).

The Father gives this ministry to the Son as an act of love (5:20), and the benefits of God's ministry through the Son result in love

---

44   Oden, *Pastoral Theology*, 80.
45   Root *The Pastor in a Secular Age*, 275.

for redeemed humanity through the beloved Son. The church experiences and receives election, adoption, redemption, and inheritance through Jesus Christ. It is united to him in his death, his resurrection, and his ascension. Consequently, it receives the Holy Spirit through the Son (Eph. 1).

If the Father, the Son, and the Spirit work together in their one nature in mutual love, so the Son asks the church to be united in Him and his ministry to the church (John 15:10; 17:22–26). Thus the old command of loving God and loving neighbor (John 14:34; 1 John 2:7) receives new strength in the command of the Son to the disciples. Love binds the Trinity together, and so our ministry and common life together as believers is to be marked by our mutual love and unity for one another (Eph. 4:1–6).

Consequently, human ministry is plural in Scripture. Adam and Eve's ministry in the world is meant to be accomplished in the plurality of being male and female and the unity of husband and wife (Gen. 2:23–24). Noah goes on the ark with his sons (Gen. 6:18; 7:6–7). Abram is called with his household (Gen. 17). Moses is partnered with his brother Aaron and his sister Miriam in the ministry of the Exodus and the wilderness (Exod. 4:14–17; 15:20–21). Joshua and Caleb urge the Israelites to take the Promised Land (Num. 14:6–9). Elijah partners with Elisha (1 Kings 19:19–21). Jesus chooses twelve disciples (Matt. 6:12–15), and the apostles choose the seven deacons (Acts 6:1–7). Paul partners with Barnabas and John Mark (Acts 13:1–2); later he partners with Silas and Timothy (Acts 15:40–16:3).

As churches are established across the eastern Roman Empire and in Rome itself, it is no surprise that Paul, Timothy, and Titus work to establish a plurality of shepherds in the churches they plant and support (1 Tim. 3; Titus 1). And it is no surprise that major theological decisions are made in groups such as the Jerusalem Council (Acts 15), the sending out of missionaries from Antioch (Acts 13:1–2), and the endorsement of Paul's mission to the Gentiles (Gal. 2:1–10).

Associate pastors, then, are participants in a plurality of ministers in their local congregations. While they are often junior partners and always subordinates to senior pastors, associates work with and alongside other pastoral staff as they jointly serve the needs of their churches. The plurality of ministerial partners reminds associates that they are not alone in their responsibilities, and that working with others requires being responsive to the gifts of ministry in others. Such a response requires mutual submission and not mere subordination. Mutual submission is marked by patience and spirit of unity given by the Holy Spirit. It is marked by love, wisdom, and grace rather than anger and division. Mutual submission is responsive to authority, but it does not seek to dominate or manipulate others, but to serve in love.

The Pastor as Gift to, and Worker in, the Church

Pastors serve numerous roles through many tasks. Pastors are spiritual caregivers, counselors, preachers of the Word, evangelists, teachers of the faith, and intercessors for the congregation. But more significant than what they do is who they are and what they are. Paul is clear that God's ministers are gifts to the church, given by the Lord Jesus to her people to serve them and prepare them for good work of ministry in a darkened world (Eph. 4:11–12). While the congregation may call a pastor, that calling confirms the calling God has already made. A pastor's ministry comes from God as a gift to the pastor (cf. Paul's own call in Ephesians 3:7) but also a gift to the congregation. Thus, whatever ministry responsibilities might be given to an associate pastor—whether youth ministry, visitation, young adults, worship, or senior adults—they are just as much pastors as the senior pastor in a congregation, because of the calling's origin in God's grace.

God and the Pastor as Divine-Human Partners in Teaching and Managing

While ministry is a divine act of the triune God and the work of people working together, it is also a divine and human partnership, where God in the ministry of the Holy Spirit enters into the human act of ministry with his presence and power. Thus ministry in any situation is God's work in and with the minister. This presence is at once bound into our unity with Jesus in the Holy Spirit and caught up in Christ's command to abide in him, as well as in God's instruction that the church reflect the divine reality of her oneness in our human practices on earth (John 17). Christians are to abide with one another and be one with one another in the Spirit's presence.

For our work, it is significant to see that God is the first teacher of the church. The prophets set an eschatological expectation that God himself will teach Israel to live in covenant relationship with him (Isa. 2:3; 54:13, Jer. 31:33–34; Mic. 4:2). God comes to Israel as her teacher in Christ (John 6:45), reveals to the church the mind of Christ through the Spirit (1 Cor. 2:10–11, 16; cf. John 14:26; 16:12), and instructs the church in brotherly love (1 Thess. 4:9). Even learning in the church is a partnership with the living God, who gives the Spirit to the whole church and speaks to the church through her various ministers (Eph. 4:11). The church is to listen to the Spirit during her orderly worship as he speaks through the whole body (1 Cor. 12–14).

God also manages in his instructions. God gives explicit details to Noah regarding the instructions for the ark (Gen. 6:14–16), to Moses for the institution and carrying out of Passover and its subsequent memorials (Exod. 12:1–28; 12:43–31:16), as well as for the building of the tabernacle (Exod. 25–31) and the cycle of Israel's worship (Lev. 1–8, 21–25). God oversees Israel's travel in the wilderness (Num. 9:15–23) and battle plans for Joshua (Josh. 6:1–5; 8:1–2) and in the New Testament directs the churches' leaders in their ministry (Acts 8:29; 9:10–17; 10:19–20; 13:1–3).

The Human Ministry of Management in Scripture

Administration is a critical part of pastoral ministry that the Bible affirms as being on par with proclamation and working wonders in the power of the Holy Spirit.

For example, Joseph by the Holy Spirit is a leader but also receives visions from God in his youth (Gen. 37:1–11) and can interpret dreams by the Holy Spirit (40:8–19; 41:16). Joseph is appointed an overseer in a variety of settings: his father appoints him to oversee his brothers (37:12–14), Potiphar sets him over his whole household (39:1–6), the jailer appoints him over Pharaoh's prison (39:20–23), and Pharaoh appoints him over all Egypt as second in command (41:37–43). Yet for Joseph, management is closely connected with saving and preserving life (41:36; 45:6–8). When Joseph interprets the dreams of the cupbearer, the baker, and Pharaoh, life and death are on the line. Joseph oversees the gathering and distribution of life-giving food both to Egypt (41:56–57) and to his father's family (47:12). When Joseph meets his brothers who betrayed him, he stewards his position of power to reconcile with his brothers, be reunited with his family, save his family, and provide a place for them to live (45:9–15; 47:1–12). He partners with God to do good in the midst of his brother's evil intentions (50:15–21).

Later Moses, after leading Israel out of Egypt, becomes the judge of all the people. Moses notes that his ministry is not merely about his wisdom but about God's justice, since "the people come to me to inquire of God; when they have a dispute, they come to me and I decide between one person and the other, and I make them know the statures of God and his laws" (Exod. 18:15–16). Moses's administration of justice depends on God and the people's desire for God's justice. The relationship Moses has with Israel and the relationship has with God matter to the management of the people. His father-in-law Jethro is concerned for Moses but also for the people, who will mutually wear out (18:17). Such ministry is too heavy for one person. So, Jethro instructs Moses to select men of good reputation who can oversee the people in orders of thousands, hundreds, fifties, and tens (18:21–23). "They will bear the burden with you. If you do this, God will direct you, you will be able to endure, and all this people also will go to their place in peace" (18:22–23). In this solution, God's relationship with the people is still front and center, Moses will endure in his ministry to the people, and God's *shalom* (peace) will be preserved.

Later, when Israel grumbles about a lack of meat (Num. 11:12–23), Moses complains to God that he is, as Jethro predicted, overwhelmed: "I am not able to carry all this people alone, the burden is too heavy for me" (11:14). In this story God is the one who instructs Moses to appoint elders for the people to assist Moses with his burden (11:17).

When Moses presents the elders, God takes the Holy Spirit—who is on Moses (11:19)—and puts it on the elders (11:17, 25). They immediately prophecy (11:25), though their primary responsibility is assisting Moses with the burden of leading and managing so many people. The ministry of management cannot be disconnected from the ministry of prophecy and provision; all ministry relies on the Holy Spirit.

In another story involving food, when there is a problem ensuring that all widows are given their necessary bread after Pentecost (cf. Acts 6:1), the apostles appoint seven deacons (servants) to make sure that this specific need is met (6:2). Yet when the apostles choose the seven and grant authority to them by laying their hands on them (6:6), they choose men of good reputation who are full of the Holy Spirit (6:3). One is Stephen, who is so full of grace and power by the Holy Spirit that he performs wonders and is a powerful preacher (Acts 6:5, 8; 7:1–53) who is reminiscent of Moses (6:15; cf. Exod. 34:34–35). Another is Philip, who also performs signs, preaches, and casts out demons (Acts 8:4–7), reminiscent of Elijah (Acts 8:39; cf. 1 Kings 18:7–12; 2 Kings 2:9–11). The ministry of management is not distant from the ministry of preaching and healing; all ministry relies on the Holy Spirit.

Moreover, Paul gives instructions to churches on how to organize their gatherings, their worship, and their leadership. He provides guidance on worship to the Corinthians by describing the purpose of tongues and prophecy (1 Cor. 14:1–24), prescribing the number of speakers (14:27–28), and determining when there should be silence and speaking (14:28, 30, 34). He gives detailed instructions on how prophecy and prayer should be done by men and women (11:1–16), and how the Lord's Supper is to be served and received (11:17–33). Yet these instructions cannot be understood without reference to the Spirit's power in the diverse spiritual gifts given to the members of Christ's body (12:1–11). "All these are empowered by one and the same Spirit, who apportions to each one individually as he wills" (12:11). Even the Spirit of God administers in the churches.

Further, Paul instructs both Timothy and Titus to appoint church leaders (1 Tim. 3:1–11; Titus 1:5–8). Timothy is explicitly told to appoint those who are good managers of their own households and who have good reputation with outsiders. In other words, Titus and Timothy are to appoint people who have godly relationships and do good to those around them. Such people are then responsible for the ministry of the Word, for preserving good doctrine, and for taking care of the needs of a host of individuals (young men, older men, younger women, and widows).

Conclusion

As seen above, the triune God remains committed to creation and the life of humanity throughout the biblical narrative. While God opposes sin and idolatry which results in death, disorder, and oppression, God is utterly committed to blessing humanity and the world. Since his commission to rule the earth and subdue it is never rescinded, humanity is still responsible to fulfill its commission in submission to God, though humanity chooses to fulfill this commission in autonomy.

Jesus Christ, the Good Shepherd, is the image of God, since in point of fact he is God, and since as a human being he demonstrates exactly who God is and what it is to follow God in one person (John 1:14). Jesus is the heir of creation; creation is the Father's gift to the Son which he shares with those he redeems. Jesus will fill all things with himself—he is the goal of all things, and in him all things hold together (Col. 1:15–20).

Thus, any human endeavor is good structurally (that is, as God created it), though all human endeavors are bent by the fall in their application. All human endeavors are redeemed in the work of Christ and find a meaningful place in God's kingdom.

Management is thus structurally good yet misapplied by human fallenness.[46] It is good in so far as it stewards life along the lines of order that God has built into his creation. It is good in so far as it honors human life, recognizes the partnership and the significance of being human, and seeks to recognize the honor of human participants. It is good in so far as it stewards the good gifts of God's creation.

---

46 Ashford and Thomas, *The Gospel of Our King*, 37.

Management participates in the fall when it sets up human autonomy in opposition to God's reign; it participates in idolatry when it sets up human beings, a process, or a goal as god. It participates in the fall when it utilizes oppression, death, or shame to accomplish its purposes and foments disorder.

Management participates in the reign of God when it recognizes that the way to life is through participation in the death of Jesus by faith, and when managers pattern their lives and practices on the life and practice of Jesus.

Therefore, management is a worthy human activity because of creation and redemption. Since God has remained committed to human life and purpose, God through common grace (the love and mercy poured out on all humanity) allows for the meaningful study of and practice of specific human activities so that human life and order may continue. Because rational and scientific activity are a part of human activity, philosophical and scientific study of managerial practices is a worthy endeavor—because they participate in the common life of human calling! Christians who therefore read and examine secular organizational and educational literature for wisdom are being responsible, so long as this literature is submitted to the reign of God, the lordship of Christ, and the life of the Spirit.

Management is not the little sibling of either human calling or pastoral ministry—it requires the presence and power of the Spirit just as preaching and all other pastoral tasks do. The ministry of management cannot be pulled apart from prophecy, preaching, or any other ministerial task or spiritual gift, let alone the presence and work of the Spirit in the Christian individually or the church corporately. All pastoral work is meant to go together. Managing is not just about task management; rather, it is about caring for real people for whom the Lord Jesus came in the flesh, died, and was risen. It is relational work. It is truly pastoral work.

As we have seen, existing research describes associate pastors as managers, and this study continues to do so. Certainly they do other tasks: visitation, counseling, preaching, discipleship, teaching, evangelizing, baptizing and serving the Lord's Supper. However, what distinguishes associate ministry from senior pastor ministry is the role of administration and management. Therefore, let us reclaim management as a pastoral task and dare to think of it as worthy of scriptural and theological reflection.

Now that we've established that management is ministerial task, and that the examination of organizational and educational literature is a responsible activity for Christians—and since relationships and learning are pivotal in management—we can turn our attention to the relational nature of management in organizations in chapter 2. Then in chapter 3, we will turn our attention to the nature of learning in organizations.

CHAPTER 2

Relationships in Organizations

I enjoy hanging pictures on my walls, so much so that my colleagues often ask for help hanging diplomas or arranging framed paintings and keepsakes. Two tools are essential to hanging a picture. The first is a measuring tape, which keeps the pictures at the same height. The second is a bubble level which keeps the pictures from being tilted and uneven. The measuring tape keeps me oriented to the floor and to other pictures already hung, and the bubble level keeps me oriented to the walls and the ceiling. Without either, the picture will be lopsided when it is hung.

This chapter examines two tools that will help us understand how relationships work in organizations. Let's think of them as essential tools to understand how organizations work. These two tools are role theory and systems thinking. These theories describe how relationships form and change in organizations, and how tensions are constructed within those relationships. The ideas in this chapter will help us as we answer the question "How do associate pastors navigate their congregational organizations?" in chapter 5.

Along the way, I will attempt to provide illustrations from my experience in associate ministry that highlight the concepts being described. I will then shift from my own experiences to the stories and experiences of the other associate pastors represented in this study.

Forming Relationships in Organizations: Role Theory and Systems Thinking

Again, the first two tools that orient us to the people and the tasks of an organization are role theory and systems thinking. We'll take a brief look at these theories as ways of trying to understand congregations, from the perspective of an associate pastor.

Role Theory

Let's begin with role theory and the concept of roles. A role is a pattern of behavior enacted by agents in a position, office, or status within an organization. Roles are created in relationship to other roles. Originally, roles were described as strict pairs such as husband and wife, salesperson and customer, employee and employer,[1] but as the field of role theory advanced, roles were seen in a complex set of interdependent relationships known as role sets.[2]

Role theorists attempted to describe how roles are formed. Initially, role theory was divided into the two camps: structuralism and symbolic interactionism. A simple way to understand the two camps is by distinguishing what they emphasize: enforced values in the case of structuralism and negotiated relationships in the case of symbolic interactionism. On one hand, structuralism held that roles are determined by an organization's norms and values, which it enforces through rewards and punishments.[3] Those who follow the norms and values get new responsibilities, promotions, and pay raises. Those who ignore them are written up, passed over for jobs, or fired. On the other hand, symbolic interactionism held that roles are constructed in interaction and negotiation between various role incumbents.[4] In later research, role theorists reconsidered how these two camps fit together. Rather than opposing camps, structuralism and symbolic interactions were really flip sides of the same coin. All roles have both normalized and value-based structures which are

---

1   Linton, Ralph. *The Study of Man*, 113.
2   Merton, "The Role Set," 110.
3   Katz and Kahn, *The Social Psychology of Organizations*.
4   Turner, "Strategy for Developing an Integrated Role Theory," 110.

constructed in dynamic relationships that allow the roles to grow, develop, and change.[5]

Let's take the ideas from these two paragraphs and apply them to the concept of an associate pastor. In Linton's original version of role theory, roles occurred in pairs. One might see how a senior pastor and an associate pastor work together in a pair. But as Merton made clear, roles don't simply happen in pairs but in larger sets of relationships. So, associate pastors would be in relationship with senior pastors, elders (or deacons, or board members), key leaders, leaders from outside the church, administrative assistants, and broader church constituents and members. Figure 2-1 below describes the way Linton and Merton thought of role theory as applied to associate pastors.

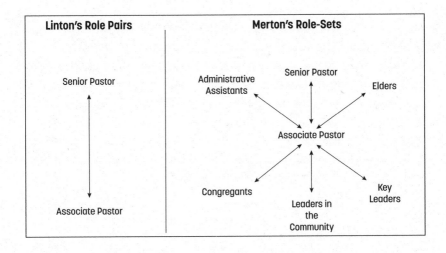

Figure 2-1: Role Pairs versus Role Sets

5   Hilbert, "Toward an Improved Understanding of 'Role'"; Bosworth and Kreps, "Structure as Process."

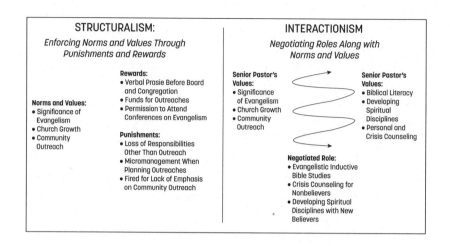

Figure 2-2: Structuralism and Interactionism

One might encounter a structural stance toward roles in a church, where the senior pastor has a command-and-control mentality toward associate staff, giving out explicit goals designed around norms and values which are rewarded with perks and bonuses or punished with micromanagement or termination. On the other hand, one might encounter an interactivist stance on roles in an organization, where the senior pastor treats associates as colleagues and not merely subordinates, and allows their perspective, talents, and experience to guide their actions in the church, as described in Figure 2-2.

Systems Thinking

If that is role theory, what about systems thinking? You can think about role theory as if the different persons in an organization were the parts of an engine in a car. Role theory takes the engine apart to examine all the gears and pistons next to one another. But systems theory examines all of these parts together *as the engine is running*. Role theory is analytic (examines the members of an organization and describes them individually) while systems thinking is synthetic (examines what all the parts are doing together as they work). Systems thinking looks at the whole system and concentrates on the complexity and of its social and organizational movement.[6] Three critical elements of systems thinking are holistic thinking, tension between process and structure, and nonlinear causation. Holistic thinking examines the entire organization and interrelation of its parts.[7] The tension between process and structure requires examining how information and activity flow between the parts and the members of the organization, and how process influences change in structure.[8] Nonlinear causation rejects linear cause-and-effect principles and instead focuses on interrelationships between all aspects of a system.[9]

Let's apply this theory to associate ministry. Holistic thinking would seek to situate the associate pastor in the entirety of the congregation and its work. What interactions and work does the associate do with the senior pastor, administrative assistant, janitor, elder board, key leaders, and nursery workers? The tension between process and structure examines how that work occurs: Does the associate pastor communicate clearly what he is doing to the senior pastor, or does he rely on the administrative assistant to pass on information? Does the associate pastor give clear updates and seek permissions from the elders, or does she simply speak with key leaders and leave them in the dark? Nonlinear causation examines how relationships impact action: the Sunday school director went over budget on curriculum supplies with the senior pastor's permission since the nursery director borrowed without asking from the supply closet, but as a result the elder board is asking everyone cut their spending by 10% across the board, which means the associate pastor can't go to the youth conference she always attends.

Bowen Family Systems (BFS) is a particular system thinking theory that has received a lot of attention because of its focus on

---

6   Jackson, *Systems Thinking*, 3; cf. Checkland, *Systems Thinking, Systems Practice*, 78–79.
7   Jackson, *Systems Thinking*, xv; Bertalanffy, *General System Theory*, 37–38; Kraft, *A Reason to Hope*, 110; cf. Bohm, *Wholeness and the Implicate Order*, 3–4, 9.
8   Friedman, *Generation to Generation*, 15–18; Senge, *The Fifth Discipline*, 73; cf. Bohm, *Wholeness and the Implicate Order*, 162.
9   Friedman, *Generation to Generation*, 15–18.

organic organizations such as families and congregations.[10] BFS focuses on how individuals form relationships to share emotional energy and strain.

BFS suggests that all systems are composed by two counterbalancing forces labeled individuality and togetherness. These forces create unity or conflict in an emotional system such as a family or congregation. These two life forces are developed through learning. In order to be healthy, it is important for family members to develop abilities where they can stand apart as individuals and belong to the emotional system at the same time,[11] and define "goals and values apart from surrounding togetherness pressures."[12] This capacity is called self-differentiation. It has three elements: nonanxious presence while remaining in the system, taking responsibility for individual emotional health, and being yourself while staying connected to a system.[13]

Two-person relational dyads are balanced by equal but changing contributions of energy from two partners. The amount of emotional energy tied into a dyad is determined by the ability of the individuals to differentiate themselves from one another by managing togetherness and individuality.[14] Anxiety is a key emotion that influences the family system. While not inherently destructive to a system, an individual's response to anxiety is critical to functioning well in a family system.[15] Anxiety has two forms: short-lived acute anxiety, and chronic anxiety that develops in response to imagined ongoing fear. Kerr and Bowen observed that chronic anxiety and differentiation of self are inversely related to one another. As chronic anxiety goes up, differentiation of self goes down and produces strain on family members' ability to adapt in a system.[16]

---

10   Steinke, *Congregational Leadership in Anxious Times;* Friedman, *Generation to Generation*; Herrington, Creech, and Taylor, *The Leader's Journey.*
11   Steinke, *Congregational Leadership in Anxious Times,* 25.
12   Friedman, *Generation to Generation,* 27.
13   Friedman, *Generation to Generation,* 25, 27.
14   Kerr and Bowen, *Family Evaluation,* 68; cf. Steinke, *Congregational Leadership in Anxious Times,* 24.
15   Steinke, *Congregational Leadership in Anxious Times,* 7.
16   Kerr and Bowen, *Family Evaluation,* 117, 112.

But what if things are unhealthy in a relationship? According to BFS, relational dyads are inherently unstable and struggle to handle anxiety, so the members look for somewhere else to put it. You may remember from shop class that triangles are the strongest shapes because of their rigidity; they can handle a lot more stress and strain. When a dyad has too much anxiety to handle, one of the members brings in another person to help them handle the relational stress.

Here's an easy example: A married couple is having a terrible fight, which ends without the issue being resolved. The husband calls his brother to process the fight and to gain emotional support for his side of the conflict. The husband just inserted his brother into the system to help deal him deal with the anxiety.

BFS calls this triangulation. Just as triangles are inherently rigid and capable of handling more load than rectangle shapes, emotional triangles can handle more anxiety by "shifting anxiety around the system."[17] While triangulating relationships is natural and individuals occupy positions in several interlocking triangles,[18] the actual task of a triangled person is to keep emotionally detached from the anxiety of the other two individuals and require them to handle their own emotional anxiety.[19] Let's go back to our married couple and the husband's brother. While the brother could empathize with the husband, he should not attempt to interfere in the relationship; the husband and the wife need to resolve their fight on their own.

Here is an example from my first church of where an anxious triangle was avoided. Remember the parent from the Introduction who hadn't completed a background check? We were essentially estranged from one another for about a year. To say that anxiety was high between us was an understatement. A caring elder spoke with the parent, and he gently came to me and suggested that I meet with

17   Kerr and Bowen, *Family Evaluation*, 135; cf. Herrington, Creech, and Taylor, *The Leader's Journey*, 52.
18   Kerr and Bowen, *Family Evaluation*, 134, 142; Herrington, Creech, and Taylor, *The Leader's Journey*, 52.
19   Herrington, Creech, and Taylor, *The Leader's Journey*, 55–57.

this parent for coffee. He didn't insert himself into the relationship, but he pushed us to resolve the conflict and anxiety.

Here is an example of an anxious triangle. One of my middle school students gave me a compliment on social media by tagging me in a meme that contained some inappropriate language. Another child's parent saw the meme and expletive. He came to my office and asked why I was tagged in this meme. Even though I couldn't control the student's actions on social media and the student was saying something positive, he was disturbed that I was mentioned. In this case, the presence of the profanity inserted enough anxiety in the system that a triangle was created between me, the parent, and the student. He transferred his anxiety to me, and I removed the tag.

Tensions in Organizations

As noted in the previous chapter, associate ministry is wrought with ambiguity, which is often perceived as role conflict and role ambiguity.[20] This ambiguity often arises in different tensions that come from being in the middle of an organization.[21]

From this introduction to role theory and systems theory, we see that associate pastors face challenges that, while not unique to associate pastoral ministry or to ministry in general, are significant for understanding their specific roles. These challenges can be described as five important tensions: the tension between the individual and the organization, the tension between organizational culture and role performance, the tension between hierarchical and asymmetrical power, the tension between leadership and followership, and the tension between role responsibilities and interpersonal relationships.

Tension 1: The Individual versus the Organization

This tension emphasizes the analytic dimension of the individual versus the synthetic relationship of the entire organization or system.

---

20   Kahn, et al., *Organizational Stress*; Rizzo, House, and Lirtzman, "Role Conflict and Ambiguity in Complex Organizations"; Van Sell, Brief, and Schuler, "Role Conflict and Role Ambiguity"; Faucett, Corwyn, and Poling, "Clergy Role Stress."
21   Oshry, *In the Middle*, 80.

This comparison places role theory in a tension with systems thinking—and individuals, particularly associate pastors, must be attentive to their own roles while also being mindful of the whole system as it changes.[22] Keeping in mind BFS, associate pastors are a part of a congregational family system[23]; they change the system by their very presence and are changed by the system itself.[24]

Here's an example from my very early days of ministry. Everyone was excited when I arrived for my first day of work, including one leader who was passionate about the middle school ministry he had developed. Other parents and leaders were also excited, since they hoped that I would change the atmosphere in this same ministry from being primarily for boys to more inclusive of girls. The middle school leader wanted a ministry that conformed to cultural expectations for rural preteen boys: free, wild, relatively unstructured. The other parents wanted a place for their young girls to feel included and with boundaries on the boys' behavior. No matter what I did, my decision would carry a lot of power, disappointing either the specific leader or the parents of the girls. In the end, I elected to pause middle school ministry for the summer until I could learn more and reset the values and expectations of the group through a reboot in the fall.

In this scenario, it's important to see all the parts of the ministry influencing each other in a synthetic way. The key leader, the other leaders, the girls, the boys, and I as the new associate pastor were all together in the system; our individual decisions impacted everyone else. However, we can also see how the individuals work analytically: they all had different needs and interests that they were hoping I would meet and honor. But the system must be put back together to form a working whole. In this instance, the parents were looking to the new associate pastor as a hope for change; the key leader was looking to me for continued empowerment and permission. But my

---

22   Mitchell, *Multiple Staff Ministries*, 50–51.
23   Friedman, *Generation to Generation*.
24   Westing, *Church Staff Handbook*, 156; Even, "Applying Systems Theory to the Entry of the Associate Pastor into a New Congregational System as Model and Means for Lay Employment," 31.

presence changed the system simply by showing up and disrupting and rebalancing the relationships. New possibilities were present when I arrived, but no matter what I did the system would be different.

Tension 2: Organizational Culture versus Role Performance

This tension involves the influence of the structure of an organization versus processes or action within the organization. Structure in this sense is about more than an organizational chart. Rather, it includes norms and values that the organization holds as important along with positions. We might call structure *organizational culture*.[25] Process, however, expresses the ability of an individual to either conform to those norms and values or improvise how he or she performs the role.[26] In other words, this tension emphasizes organizational expectations on the structure side and the response of the individual to those expectations on the other side. In congregations, associate pastors must respond to church values and norms but may have freedom to improvise their roles according to their gifts and talents in response to congregational needs or opportunities.

At one of my churches, the senior pastor opted to eliminate a late evening Christmas Eve service for a more family-friendly late afternoon service, with a spontaneous nativity scene created on the spot by asking children who came with their families to act out the drama of the Christmas story. While parents appreciated a service that accommodated families with young children, senior members and families with older children missed the more traditional candlelight service later in the evening that they had always come to expect. After listening to several families and with the senior pastors' permission, I developed the "expected" Christmas Eve carol sing with "Silent Night" and short homily as a "response" to the desires of a portion of the congregation. Structure and action coincide and respond to one another.

---

25   Livermore, *Cultural Intelligence*, 97–98.
26   Bosworth and Kreps, "Structure as Process," 700–704.

Tension 3: Hierarchical versus Asymmetrical Power

Artists sometime refer to imbalance in paintings, sculptures, and architecture as asymmetry when the elements of the artwork are arranged without reference to a particular line of symmetry. For example, Greek and Roman temples have a mirrored symmetry; the right side of the building is the mirror of the left side down a center line. However, twentieth-century architects often created buildings where the balance in the composition did not depend on mirror symmetry; the left and right were not balanced along a centerline.

Associate pastors must negotiate tensions of power, or "the capacity to act," in all their relationships.[27] Most organizations have a hierarchy, which is sometimes directive and based on rules, patterns, and roles.[28] However, sometimes leaders share roles and power collaboratively with followers, sometimes allowing followers to lead.[29] When this happens, power and relationships become asymmetrical. They are no longer about hierarchy but about cooperation.

Associate pastors usually have asymmetrical relationships of power with role sets that they must negotiate responsibly.[30] Collaborative ministry requires rejecting default assumptions about submission and dominance and learning genuine cooperation.[31] It also requires that we remember that asymmetry may come about from different gifts and talents, and that asymmetrical relationships are not necessarily wicked or bad.[32]

Here's a clear example. At my second church, even though I was the associate pastor, my senior pastor used to describe me as the "senior pastor of youth ministry, adult education, and small groups." He was clearly the senior pastor to whom I reported. But he allowed me the power along with the responsibility to act within my specific

---

27   Cervero and Wilson, *Planning Responsibly for Adult Education*, 29.
28   Hollander, *Leadership Dynamics*, 11, 17–18.
29   Forester, "Learning from Practice in the Face of Conflict and Integrating Technical Expertise with Participatory Planning," 344.
30   Cervero and Wilson, *Planning Responsibly for Adult Education*, 127.
31   Prickard *Theological Foundations for Collaborative Ministry*, 3; cf. Overman, "Associate Pastor as Collaborator," 11.
32   Burns, Chapman, Guthrie, *The Politics of Ministry*, 47.

ministries, as long as I operated with the core guiding principles and values of the church's ministry in mind. On occasion, however, he would step in and direct me in a hierarchical fashion. For example, one time he had discovered a new form of performance art called PechaKucha, and asked me to develop a summer adult education series on Proverbs using PechaKucha as the format.

Tension 4: Leadership versus Followership

Leadership and followership are in tension with each other in organizations, though both revolve around the purposes of the organization.[33] On one side of this dynamic, power lies with the leader to control the follower; on the other side, the follower has power to influence the leader. Followership examines how followers develop their roles in relationship to leaders. There are two primary approaches to followership. The first has its roots in a role-based approach to role theory; the second has an interactionist approach to role theory. The role-based approach places emphasis on the follower's role to push the leader to conform to the needs of the organization. The interactionist approach describes how the follower and the senior pastor negotiate to agreed-upon roles and responsibilities.[34] Leadership and followership thus mutually influence one another.[35] Associate pastors can occupy both the position of leader and follower at the same time.[36]

At one of my churches, I served as a nonvoting elder on the board. In this role, it was my responsibility as a follower to help clarify the vision of the church with the senior pastor. At one point, the board held congregation-wide listening sessions to discern what the future goals of the church ought to be. I led many of the sessions and wrote a summary of each future action for the senior pastor and the elders. After reviewing the feedback, the senior pastor and the elders appointed a working group to create a proposal for the church's future. I cowrote a long report with the working group chair. The

---

33   Chaleef, *The Courageous Follower*, 2–3.
34   Uhl-Bien, et al., "Followership Theory," 89.
35   Kelley, *The Power of Followership*, 34.
36   Bonem and Patterson, *Leading from the Second Chair*, 25–26.

senior pastor responded to the group's proposal with his own suggestions which I, the senior pastor, and the elders debated until we came to agreement. Throughout the process, the senior pastor and I had some intense but honest conversations about the church's future just between the two of us. In this situation, I practiced followership by helping my senior pastor (and the elders) come to a consensus about the church's future.

Also at my second church, my senior pastor and I worked to develop roles and boundaries with one another. For example, he was very insistent that my specific adult Sunday school class always study a book of the Bible, as opposed a specific popular theology book or current issue. This was a firm line for him. At the same time, though, I pushed him to allow me to develop a young adult group with the help of several mid-aged adults. In this sense, one of my roles was to create new-frontier ministries. He was comfortable with this role, as long as I didn't overtax myself and didn't depend on him for too much oversight or support.

Tension 5: Role Responsibilities versus Interpersonal Relationships

Organizations have a tension between expected patterns of role behavior and freedom to develop relationships beyond those expectations. On the one side of this tension, organization has power to reward conformity to those patterns. On the other side of the tension, the power lies in the persons within the relationship to determine the boundaries of the relationships.

Organizations exist in a tension between rational patterns of interaction defined by role and status on one end and interpersonal dynamics on the other. On one hand, organizations are patterned motivated acts of human beings,[37] which require learning, accepting, and fulfilling expectations. Value systems bind organizations together through corresponding rewards and punishments.[38]

---

37   Katz and Kahn, *The Social Psychology of Organizations*, 187–88.
38   Katz and Kahn, *The Social Psychology of Organizations*, 8, 41–43.

On the other hand, role development is influenced by identity, power and influence, needs and goals, and acceptance and intimacy.[39] Individuals and organizations are reciprocal; employees are not simply technically competent workers but relational interpersonal beings in their organizations.[40] This tension explores how people meet their organization's goals and values versus how their personal and relational needs and values are met within the organization.

Let's frame this tension with three questions: Which comes first in a church—the organizational goals or the relationships between the players? Which has priority for associate pastors—their personal friendship with their senior pastors or their senior pastor's expectations as their superiors? Is it good to have close relationships with board members or key leaders, or is some relational distance required to make work feasible?

Conclusion

Organizations are made of complicated relationships based on roles and rules, but also based on freedom, performance, and power. These relationships experience a number of significant and important tensions that can be themselves and ambiguous and difficult to navigate. Certainly church relationships, while brought together by the Holy Spirit, also contain their own relational complexities and ambiguities, which will be explored in chapter 5. In the next chapter, we turn our attention to how learning happens in organizations, both individually and across the whole organization.

---

39   Schein, *Organizational Culture and Leadership*, 149.
40   Argyris, *Interpersonal Competence and Organizational Effectiveness*, 9–21.

CHAPTER 3

Learning in Organizations

My family currently goes to a very liturgical church. Every week, the elders and pastors stop and explain the how and why behind each piece of the liturgy, from the orienting prayer to the passing of the peace to the prayers of the people. They're very conscientious about ensuring that the congregation remembers the reasons for the liturgical steps and that newcomers understand what is happening in the service.

Our church's liturgy illustrates a form of organizational learning. Organizational learning occurs when one person in an organization passes information and learning onto other members throughout the system. Notice that organizational learning cannot occur without an individual taking the initiative to learn on their own agenda to improve the organization.

Let's look closer at an example from the last chapter: My senior pastor encountered PechaKucha at a local restaurant. He was fascinated, so he did some research and invited me and two other leaders to a PechaKucha gathering. Afterward, he taught us the rules of the format, and I and these other leaders taught others to execute a PechaKucha. This team them utilized the format for a summer adult education class. Lee was the first in. He learned, but then he shared his learning with others to infect the church with an obsession with PechaKucha.

Pastoral ministry has always had teaching and learning near its center, and once again associate ministry is no exception to this paradigm. While existing literature describes associate pastors as managers,

I would argue that a facilitator of learning paradigm is a better model for associates than a command-and-control model. Facilitators of learning are responsible for both their own individual learning and for spreading learning around their organizations.

In the last chapter, we started to build a toolbox of helpful organizational theories to provide a map on how relationships form and work in organizations. In this chapter, we will expand that toolbox as we explore how individual and organizational learning work in organizations. This information informs the themes and categories that we will encounter in chapters 6 and 7 on how associate pastors facilitate their own learning and the learning of others in their organization. In chapter 4, we will apply both chapters 2 and 3 to the position of the associate pastor as a facilitator of learning.

Let's now add three additional tools to the toolbox. Learning in organizations requires an understanding of (1) theories of action, (2) beliefs and mental models, (3) and individual learning and organizational learning.

Theories of Action

I married a farmer's daughter. At family dinners, it doesn't take long for the conversation to turn to whether or not "red" (International Harvester) or "green" (John Deere) farm equipment runs better, whether or not a certain way of ploughing a field is the optimum way to go, or whether or not planting all corn or diversifying into soybeans is a good option this year based on grain prices. Farmers are very passionate about their methods and plans for running a farm.

Whether my in-laws know it or not, their farming strategies are what scholars call *theories of action*. A theory of action is a set of beliefs about how to best perform skills in a specific discipline in order to explain, predict, and control outcomes. These skills are rooted in the practitioners' beliefs about themselves, their practice, and their environment.[1]

Pastors also have theories of action for how they go about ministry. For example, many evangelical pastors are passionate about expository

---

1   Argyris and Schön, *Theory in Practice*, 5, 7.

preaching, the importance of small groups, or teaching inductive Bible studies. Their commitment to these specific practices comes from their beliefs of the importance of hearing what the Bible says and allowing it to transform a person or community lives. However, scholars also suggest that practitioners of specific disciplines often utilize two theories of action. The first theory is an *espoused* or *explicit theory*; the second is a *theory-in-use*.[2] A theory-in-use is often a means of maintaining power and constancy in "specific variables" of practice in a practitioner's worldview and beliefs.[3]

Here is an example of an espoused theory that operated as an actual theory-in-use. One of my senior pastors firmly believed that the church should be training younger adults to become elders. The church was close to a seminary, and there were many students who were being trained for ministry, so why not give them experience on an elder board before becoming pastors? He influenced our board to always have a member under the age of thirty as an active voting elder. The practice of appointing a twentysomething (the theory-in-use) closely aligned with the espoused theory.

But as we've seen, theories-in-use don't always align with espoused theories. For example, one of my churches participated in a church softball league. The goal of the league was to allow congregants who regularly attended Sunday worship a chance to play in a fun but competitive league. Several churches, however, regularly allowed players who either didn't attend church or attended only sporadically to play as "ringers," to stack their teams and dominate the league. Because the league didn't enforce the rule, the theory-in-use did not match the espoused theory (to the great frustration of many church teams that followed the rules).

Beliefs and Mental Models

Since theories of action are rooted in beliefs, systems of beliefs called *mental models* are integral to individual and organizational

---

2   Argyris and Schön, *Theory in Practice*, 6–7.
3   Argyris and Schön, *Theory in Practice*, 15.

learning.[4] Mental models are explicit or implicit[5] assumptions or deeply held beliefs[6] built from a combination of memory and learning[7] that can allow or restrict new ideas from influencing action.[8] Mental models govern how different individuals see and interpret events.[9]

Individuals, communities, and organizations have mental models. Indeed, a leader's particular mental model is linked to the shared mental model of an organization.[10] Schein drives this last point home: "All group learning ultimately reflects someone's original beliefs and values, his or her sense of what ought to be, as distinct from what is."[11] A leader's mental model is particularly significant as it creates a framework (a theory of action) to respond to problems and becomes a shared mental model by the organization.[12]

Congregations and pastors also have mental models, and they are often a combination of implicit or explicit beliefs. Explicit congregational mental models can be found in two places. The first place is the congregation's statement of faith or doctrinal commitments, whether they are embodied in an ancient creed, a confession of faith, or a doctrinal statement. Yet keep in mind that creedal statements are explicit only in terms of a congregation's theological commitments; they do not necessarily explicitly connect doctrine to church practices. The second place is often in a congregation's statements of their vision, mission, and core values, if one exists.

---

4   Kim, "The Link between Individual and Organizational Learning"; Senge, *The Fifth Discipline*; Ellinger, "An Examination of Managers' Beliefs about Their Roles and Facilitators of Learning."
5   Kim, "The Link between Individual and Organizational Learning," 39.
6   Ellinger and Bostrom, "An Examination of Managers' Beliefs about Their Roles and Facilitators of Learning," 148.
7   Kim "The Link between Individual and Organizational Learning," 37, 39.
8   Kim "The Link between Individual and Organizational Learning," 39; Senge, *The Fifth Discipline*, 163.
9   Senge, *The Fifth Discipline*, 164.
10 Schein, *Organizational Culture and Leadership*; Kim, "The Link between Individual and Organizational Learning"; Senge, *The Fifth Discipline*; Kim and Senge, "Putting Systems into Practice"; Ellinger and Bostrom, "An Examination of Managers' Beliefs about Their Roles and Facilitators of Learning."
11 Schein, *Organizational Culture and Leadership*, 25.
12 Schein, *Organizational Culture and Leadership*, 26.

These statements may be explicit in terms of values driving practice. Often though, these core values are generated by the work of a specific pastor who is imparting his beliefs and values (his mental model) to the congregation in a working framework for ministry (a theory-of-action).

Also remember that mental models often are implicit or have implicit components that may be understated or unstated altogether. For example, while it was never explicitly stated anywhere in any literature, one of my churches had an implicit value of supporting a local youth parachurch organization. The implicit belief was that the church's youth ministry depended on a good connection to this specific ministry because it provided a place of leadership for athletic students. When I reached out to nonathletic teenagers at the fringes of the community, I was met with resistance from key leaders, students, and my church leadership, since ministry to such students neglected the relationship with this specific ministry.

As Schein noted above, a congregation's mental model is deeply informed by its pastors' mental models. These shepherds share their mental models with the congregation, and that informs and influences the congregation's own shared mental model.

Individual Learning and Organizational Learning

In order to share beliefs, organizations must promote both individual learning and organizational learning.

Learning occurs in a variety of ways and at a variety of levels both within an individual and throughout an organization. On the one hand, individual learning can be thought of as intentional and informed skill acquisition[13] or competence in a skill.[14] It can also be thought of as increased effectiveness in action,[15] which is informed

---

13   Kim, "The Link between Individual and Organizational Learning," 38.
14   Swieringa and Wierdsma, *Becoming a Learning Organization*, 19.
15   Kim, "The Link between Individual and Organizational Learning," 38.

by skill, will, and personality.[16] It can also be change of behavior,[17] which is linked to results.[18]

On the other hand, organizational learning is a collaborative process; scholars describe it with diverse terms such as relational,[19] collective,[20] social,[21] and negotiated.[22] However, individual and organizational learning have the same goals. If individual learning is about new behavior, so also organizational learning is also about teaching and acquiring new behaviors.[23] However, this learning improves performance throughout the organization.[24] Organizational learning attempts to correct action while managing affective or emotional behavior.[25] Most relevant for our study, organizational learning also requires managers to develop new perspectives on their work.[26]

Here is an example of skill acquisition at both an individual and organizational level: The worship director at my second church was constantly looking for experienced sound board technicians to help monitor the equipment and the musicians' volume and balance on Sunday mornings. She learned how to use the sound board herself, but she also then oversaw the instruction of all the technicians so that they too might be able to use the sound board effectively. Her learning was individual, but she translated that skill acquisition to a larger group of people.

Here, in turn, is an example of affective learning at the individual and organizational level: You may remember from the last chapter that one of my churches went through an intense evaluation of our values and practices. The senior pastor, based on his own personal study of Scripture and church history, became convinced that the

---

16   Swieringa and Wierdsma, *Becoming a Learning Organization*, 19.
17   Swieringa and Wierdsma, *Becoming a Learning Organization*, 19.
18   Swieringa and Wierdsma, *Becoming a Learning Organization*, 20.
19   Nonaka, "A Dynamic Theory of Organizational Knowledge Creation," 15.
20   Swieringa and Wierdsma, *Becoming a Learning Organization*, 35.
21   Watkins and Marsick, 9.
22   Wenger, *Communities of Practice*, 53–54.
23   Slater and Narver, "Market Orientation and Organizational Learning," 63.
24   Swieringa and Wierdsma, *Becoming a Learning Organization*, 19.
25   Slater and Narver, "Market Orientation and Organizational Learning," 66.
26   Slater and Narver, "Market Orientation and Organizational Learning," 66.

metaphor that ought to drive all of our practices as a church was the metaphor of home. He chose this metaphor as a corrective antidote to a perceived business mentality in the congregations around our church. He then wrote extensively on the idea of home to the elder board, discussed these ideas at length at board meetings, and insisted our language as a church reflect this metaphor in our worship practices and atmosphere. He even changed the foyer to have more seating areas that felt like a living room and changed the church's logo to contain an image of a house. Lee was convinced of the metaphor in his own learning, but he translated that idea in the way he communicated it to the board and the congregation.

Levels of Learning

Not all learning is the same. There is a difference between learning a skill and learning an orientation toward a particular discipline or practice. Every architect learns how to draw plans and build models. Not every architect shares the same philosophy or the same environment, whether rural or urban, tropical or mountainous. The conditions of the environment, specific beliefs about design, and the needs of specific clients inform how architects must learn to create new buildings.

One might think about both individual and organizational learning based on the purpose or level of the learning. Both individuals and organizations can reflect on what they are learning, how they are learning it, and why they are learning it. Theorists sometimes make distinctions between informative (changes what we know) and transformative (how we know),[27] instrumental learning (learning to control and manipulate conditions in task-oriented or performance-based work) and communicative learning (understanding what others mean),[28] as well as between technical and adaptive changes.[29]

---

27   Kegan "What 'Forms' Transform?" 50.
28   Mezirow, "Learning to Think Like an Adult," 8.
29   Heifetz, Grashow, and Linsky, *The Practice of Adaptive Leadership*, 19–23.

Some scholars describe multiple layers of reflective learning that deepen with experience; such models are referred to as learning loops (cf. Table 3-1 for various examples). The best-known model is that of Argyris and Schön, who distinguish between single-loop learning and double-loop learning.[30] Single-loop learning is an instrumental adaptation in practice in the organizational environment. Double-loop learning reflects an adaptive change in the environment itself, which involves a change in values or beliefs. While other scholars structure learning loops differently, what connects their theories is the emphasis on a cyclical relationship between theory and practice where mental models and skill and performance mutually influence one another.[31]

Table 3-1. Variations of Individual and Organizational Learning Loops

Author(s)	Single-Loop	Double-Loop	Triple-Loop
Argyris and Schon 1996	Task performance	Change in environment	Enhancing single- and double-loop learning
Swieringa and Wierdsma 1992	Learning at the rules level	Learning at insight level	Principle level
Song and Chermack 2008; Senge 1990; Slater and Narver 1995	Adaptive learning	Generative learning	Transformative learning (Song and Chermack)
Hawkins 1995	Efficiency	Effectiveness	Service

---

30   Argyris and Schön, *Organizational Learning II*, 20–21.
31   Swieringa and Wierdsma, *Becoming a Learning Organization*, 14–15.

Here are examples of single- and double-loop learning in pastoral ministry. While in seminary, I was firmly convinced that only males should be pastors. I believed this when I entered seminary, and the books I read reaffirmed this position. I had new theological skills, and I used these skills to defend my position. Acquiring these skills was a technical or instrumental form of learning; it was single-loop learning. Then, I received a wellness checkup from a female doctor. When she discovered I was in seminary, she asked, "Oh! So, does your denomination ordain women?"

I was surprised by her question. When I told her no, she replied, "Aw. Why not?" I had never met a person for whom the question was truly personal, and it really threw me for a loop—both emotionally and educationally. I entered my first church with a far more tentative position on women in ministry. Then I met a female youth minister who I greatly admired and respected, precisely because she was an outstanding pastor. I went back to Scripture, searching for a way to resolve my response to my environment. I read different books and revisited my old resources with new eyes. After about three years, I came to believe that women should be ordained as pastors. This adaptive learning forced me to rethink my church experience, my approach to Scripture, and how I would understand the nature of pastoral ministry.

Experience and Learning

Personal and organizational learning loops reflect the nature of learning from experience. Educational theorists have long known that experience, including organizational experience, goes hand-in-hand with learning.[32] In fact, a learner's experiences are a great resource for educators, if the learner is willing to tap into them.[33] Further, experience is linked to the learner's self-identity[34] and is a way of making meaning and belief.[35]

---

32 Merriam and Bierema, *Adult Learning*, 105–6, 115.
33 Knowles, Holton, and Swanson, *The Adult Learner*, 64–65.
34 Knowles, Holton, and Swanson, *The Adult Learner*, 64.
35 Cranton, *Understanding and Promoting Transformative Learning*, 19; cf. Kolb, *Experiential Learning*.

Kolb sees experiential learning as an adaption of the person to their environment.[36] All learning is "tension- and conflict-filled process"[37] that occurs as a dialectic between reflection and action.[38] Consequently, learning is a process whereby one begins by naming beliefs, testing them, and integrating new ideas as beliefs. Adaptation occurs when tensions are resolved by the process of naming, testing, and integrating new ideas in response to a person's environment.[39]

Thus learning involves transactions between the person and the environment.[40] The transaction involves both the internal "subjective" experiences as well as the "objective" environmental experiences. "These two forms of experience interpenetrate and interrelate in very complex ways."[41] The process of this interaction between environment and person creates knowledge[42] in such a way that Kolb defines learning as "the process whereby knowledge is created through the transformation of experience."[43] In other words, experience yields knowledge; knowledge is never independent of experience.[44] Such transformation of experience occurs in both the person and the environment and is continuous—"all learning is relearning" in a cyclical process of reflection.[45]

Pete Ward describes several versions of reflection cycles, including Cardijin's see-judge-act cycle; Bullard and Pritchard's learning-action, experience, theological reflection cycle; and Osmer's four-tasks paradigm (What is going on, why is this going on, what should be going on, how might one respond?). All are cycles that demand theological reflection on experience.[46] Branson and Martínez describe how this cycle of learning from experience occurs in a congregation:

---

36 Kolb, *Experiential Learning*, 31.
37 Kolb, *Experiential Learning*, 30.
38 Kolb, *Experiential Learning*, 29.
39 Kolb, *Experiential Learning*, 30–31.
40 Kolb, *Experiential Learning*, 34.
41 Kolb, *Experiential Learning*, 35.
42 Kolb, *Experiential Learning*, 36–37.
43 Kolb, *Experiential Learning*, 38.
44 Kolb, *Experiential Learning*, 38.
45 Kolb, *Experiential Learning*, 28.
46 Ward, *Introducing Practical Theology*, 97–99.

So in a church, praxis is the constant rhythm that includes study and reflection (including working with theology and other theoretical material) in continual interaction with engagement and action. A church's capacity to discern and participate in God's will is increased whenever this rhythm is well resourced and intentional.[47]

Critical Thinking as Necessary for Deeper Learning

Essential for double- and triple-loop learning is the ability to practice critical thinking. Critical thinking links values to actions[48] to ensure that action or behavior come from "some notion of good and desirability."[49] Critical thinking involves hunting and checking assumptions, taking different viewpoints, and taking informed action.[50] While assumptions can be paradigmatic (about how one views the world), prescriptive (what one thinks ought to happen), or causal (about why things happen),[51] assumptions are often taken for granted.[52]

While critical thinking is about taking action, it is not simply a rational endeavor.[53] As Brookfield states, "Reflectivity involves reasoning and/or intuition. Both are significantly influenced by conditioned emotional responses."[54] He continues:

However, as soon as you understand critical thinking to be linked to action you enter the realm of values, because you have to ask the questions, "Action for what?" and "Whose action do we want to support?"[55]

---

47   Branson and Martínez, *Churches, Cultures, and Leadership*, 41–42.
48   Brookfield, *Teaching for Critical Thinking*, 14.
49   Brookfield, *Teaching for Critical Thinking*, 15.
50   Brookfield, *Teaching for Critical Thinking*, 11–12.
51   Brookfield, *Teaching for Critical Thinking*, 17–18.
52   Mezirow, "Learning to Think Like an Adult," 9.
53   Brookfield, *Teaching for Critical Thinking*, 14.
54   Brookfield, *Teaching for Critical Thinking*, 21.
55   Brookfield, *Teaching for Critical Thinking*, 14.

In other words, critical thinking is tied to ethics as it links action to moral ends.[56] But because we spend time working to understand assumptions in relationships, we also see that we are discerning action and ethics in the context of complex relationships.

Transformative Learning

Transformative learning is helpful to the paradigm of individual and organizational because it has both "individual and social dimensions and implications."[57] Transformative learning is normally described as a ten-step process:

1. A disorienting dilemma
2. Self-examination
3. Critical assessment of assumptions
4. Recognition that one's discontent and the process of transformation are shared with others
5. Exploring options for new roles, relationships, and actions
6. Planning a new course of action
7. Acquiring knowledge and skills for implementing one's plans
8. Provisional trying of new roles
9. Building competence and self-confidence in new roles and relationships
10. A reintegration into one's life on the basis of conditions dictated by one's new perspective[58]

Mezirow describes learning in four ways: elaborating an existing frame of reference, leaning new frames of reference, transforming points of view, and transforming habits of mind.[59] A habit of mind is a pattern that relates to how knowledge is acquired and used. Such habits are not easy to change and are tied to our personality: "they are

---

56 Brookfield, *Teaching for Critical Thinking*, 15.
57 Mezirow, "Learning to Think Like an Adult," 8.
58 Mezirow, "Learning to Think Like an Adult," 22.
59 Mezirow, "Learning to Think Like an Adult," 19.

long held and deeply valued ways of seeing ourselves."[60] Since habits of mind are "unexamined,"[61] a reflective person must learn to reflect on content, process, and premises or beliefs.[62]

Critical reflection and transformative learning go hand in hand. Mezirow suggests that critical reflection is essential for reframing one's own assumptions (individual learning) and thinking about the assumptions of others (which is necessary for organizational learning). Such critical reflection can focus on personal narratives, organizations and systems, feelings and interpersonal relationships, and one's own learning.[63] Mezirow writes:

> Critical reflection, discourse, and reflective action always exist in the real world in complex, institutional, interpersonal, and historical settings, and these inevitably significantly influence the possibilities for transformative learning and shape its nature.[64]

Because transformative learning takes place in a space or time of disorientation, learning in these moments might become uncomfortable or awkward.[65] Moving toward change in a transformative moment may require identifying and managing three barriers to change: personal barriers, social/relational barriers, and cultural beliefs and practices.[66] Overcoming these barriers emphasizes the personal agency of learners to change, and imagines a new and better future for themselves if they grow and change.[67]

60   Cranton, *Understanding and Promoting Transformative Learning*, 24–25.
61   Cranton, *Understanding and Promoting Transformative Learning*, 29.
62   Cranton, *Understanding and Promoting Transformative Learning*, 34–35.
63   Mezirow, "Learning to Think Like an Adult," 23.
64   Mezirow, "Learning to Think Like an Adult," 24.
65   Elmer and Elmer, *The Learning Cycle*, 132.
66   Elmer and Elmer, *The Learning Cycle*, 112.
67   Elmer and Elmer, *The Learning Cycle*, 113.

Linking Individual Learning to the Group's Learning

Linking individual and organizational learning is critical to influencing practice and action,[68] but how does this happen? After all, while anyone in an organization can learn, his or her learning may not intentionally and purposefully spread throughout the organization.[69] Three things are necessary to ensure individual learning is passed on: first, a shared mental model (that is, shared beliefs and values); second, an educational system in which the mental models become shared; and third, committed individuals acting on the part of the organization, particularly as teachers.

Since mental models are formed in learning, they function as the link between individual and organizational learning, as organizations rely on shared mental models to provide guidance to action. Shared mental models exert pressure on individual mental models, but individual models can change shared models.[70] However, these models may be tacit, and reflect an organization's theory-in-use more than its espoused theory.[71]

As noted above, organizational learning often begins with a "mismatch" between an expected result and actual outcomes, which are resolved through reflection and action that may lead to (1) a shift in member's understanding of the organization or the task of the organization, (2) a clarification of theory of action, or (3) a new understanding of the learner's relationship to the organization.[72] These results occur as a conceptual relearning that revises the mental model of the individual but also changes conditions in the organization.[73]

However, shared mental models are insufficient for linking individual learning to organizational learning.[74] While learning is a relational process, organizations create systems that either facilitate

---

68   Argyris and Schön, *Organizational Learning II*, 6.
69   Argyris and Schön, *Organizational Learning II*, 11.
70   Kim and Senge, "Putting Systems into Practice," 281.
71   Kim and Senge, "Putting Systems into Practice," 279.
72   Argyris and Schön, *Organizational Learning II*, 11, 15–16.
73   Kim, "The Link between Individual and Organizational Learning," 40.
74   Kim and Senge, "Putting Systems into Practice," 280.

or limit learning. Such systems are made up of channels of communication, informational systems, spatial environments, procedures and routines, and systems of incentives; all of which impact how individuals can ask questions and learn.[75] These systems should facilitate learning, knowledge creation, and leadership.[76]

Examples of such systems in congregations include formal educational settings like Sunday schools, ABFs, small groups, and even Sunday worship; but they also consist of formal gatherings like board meetings, congregational meetings, committees, and formal training sessions for leaders.

Organizational learning is impossible without committed members acting on behalf of the organization.[77] Managers of the organization must be committed to the organization's mission by acting as learners and teachers. The roles of teachers[78]; "intraprenuers"[79]; and middle-up-down managers, who synthesize the vision and direction of top managers with lower-level managers' processes,[80] have been suggested for managers.

Let's review the ideas we've gone over in organizational learning. People learn in organizations, and their learning cannot be separated from their organizational experiences. Their experience in organizations impacts their own self-identity: beliefs and meaning on who they are that have already been formed in their experiences. Learning thus happens from experience to create identity and values, then changes behavior as well as competency in skills and action. This individual knowledge, if it is linked to organizational learning, can be transmitted through the organization to change skills, behavior, and attitudes and self-perception in others. It is important to note that individual learning in organizations does not automatically mean that the whole organization has learned; the individual learning must

75 Argyris and Schön, *Organizational Learning II*, 28–29.
76 Nonaka and von Krough, "Tacit Knowledge and Knowledge Conversion," 647.
77 Argyris and Schön, *Organizational Learning II*, 11.
78 French and Bazalgette, "From 'Learning Organization' to 'Teaching-Learning Organization'?" 114.
79 Molina and Callahan, "Fostering Organizational Performance," 390, 392.
80 Nonaka, "Toward Middle-Up-Down Management," 30.

be spread to the other organizational members and change the mental models and beliefs of the organizational members.

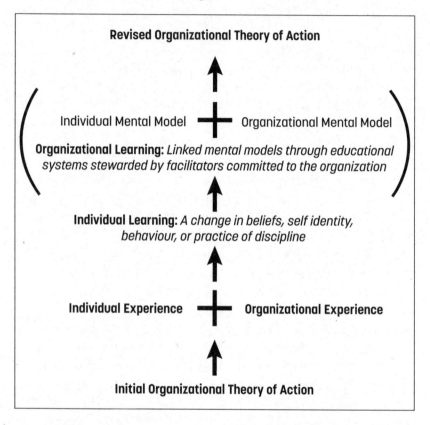

**Figure 3-1: How Theories-of-Action Are Revised
in an Organization Through Learning**

Facilitators of Learning

As we have seen, a committed member who can act as an educator is critical to helping shape the beliefs of an organization. Such a person will be recognized by a new type of manager as a facilitator of learning.[81] This person is sometimes referred to as

---

81   Ellinger, Watkins, and Bostrom, "Managers as Facilitators of Learning in Learning

a coach.[82] Facilitators of learning are tasked with helping others achieve their organizational goals[83] by programming learning to enhance creativity.[84] Facilitative leadership shifts away from viewing management as command-and-control to viewing it as developing people.[85] Such shifts may require managers to rethink their professional identity,[86] as they change their beliefs and mental models to lean into that identity.[87] Facilitative leadership is the opposite of impositional leadership,[88] and could be described as "helping people in groups transform themselves, their community, and their world."[89] Facilitative leadership has been practiced in social work,[90] local government,[91] schools,[92] libraries,[93] and architectural planning.[94]

Schwarz names four types of facilitative leaders: consultants, coaches, trainers, and leaders.[95] While facilitators are typically third-party content experts and process experts, and sometimes ex-

Organizations"; Ellinger and Bostrom, "An Examination of Managers' Beliefs about Their Roles and Facilitators of Learning."

82   Ellinger and Bostrom, "Managerial Coaching Behaviors in Learning Organizations"; Ellinger, "Antecedents and Consequences of Coaching Behavior"; cf. Hargrove, *Masterful Coaching.*

83   Guastello, "Facilitative Style, Individual Innovation, and Emergent Leadership in Problem Solving Groups," 226.

84   Guastello, "Facilitative Style, Individual Innovation, and Emergent Leadership in Problem Solving Groups," 227.

85   Ellinger, Watkins, and Bostrom, "Managers as Facilitators of Learning in Learning Organizations," 106.

86   Ellinger and Bostrom, "An Examination of Managers' Beliefs about Their Roles and Facilitators of Learning," 159.

87   Ellinger and Bostrom, "An Examination of Managers' Beliefs about Their Roles and Facilitators of Learning," 148.

88   Fryer, "Facilitative Leadership," 26.

89   Hargrove, *Masterful Coaching,* 15.

90   Breshears and Volker, *Facilitative Leadership in Social Work Practice.*

91   Svara, *Facilitative Leadership in Local Government*; Greasley and Stoker, "Mayors and Urban Governance."

92   Töremen, "A Study of Facilitative Leadership Behavior and Its Role in the Success of Schools."

93   Moore, "Facilitative Leadership."

94   Forester, "Learning from Practice in the Face of Conflict and Integrating Technical Expertise with Participatory Planning."

95   Schwarz, *The Skilled Facilitator,* 41.

empt from decision-making, a facilitative leader role is challenging because as an organizational member, "he needs to use his facilitative skills at the same time that he has strong views about the issue being discussed." [96] Facilitative leaders need not be formal leaders of organizations; the key is that they are able to help others "learn how to learn."[97]

Schwarz suggests that facilitation has four core values: valid information, free and informed choice, internal commitment to choice, and compassion.[98] Facilitators model the connection between individual and organizational learning via shared core values: "the same core values that increase your effectiveness as facilitator increase the group's effectiveness."[99] Hargrove's coaching values include stewardship, personal transformation, and reinvention, creating communities of commitment and team collaboration, and expanding people's capacity to take effective action.[100]

Facilitative learning seems akin to the eight elements for andragogy or adult learning: (1) preparing learners, (2) climate, (3) planning, (4) diagnosis of needs, (5) setting of objectives, (6) describing learning plans, (7) learning activities, and (8) evaluation.[101] At the heart of andragogy is a mechanism for mutual planning by learners and a facilitator, formed through mutual ascent, and mutual negotiation.[102]

Guthrie describes a teaching pedagogy which he names facilitated agency. "Facilitated agency includes elements of coaching, mentoring, collaboration, and formation, but ultimately emerges as a more than just the sum of these approaches." Guthrie defines facilitation as "wise guidance" while agency is "responsible image bearing." He goes on to describe facilitated agency as an integral pedagogy that harmonizes participants, methods, process, and outcomes.[103] Facilitated agency is

---

96 Schwarz, *The Skilled Facilitator*, 44.
97 Schwarz, *The Skilled Facilitator*, 327.
98 Schwarz, *The Skilled Facilitator*, 46–47.
99 Schwarz, *The Skilled Facilitator*, 48.
100 Hargrove, *Masterful Coaching*, 18, 20, 23, 25.
101 Knowles, Holton, and Swanson, *The Adult Learner*, 115–16.
102 Knowles, Holton, and Swanson, *The Adult Learner*, 115.
103 Guthrie, "Facilitated Agency," 162, 163–65.

rooted in explicitly Christian theological themes including creation, Sabbath, Christology, and discipleship. It serves as a helpful framework for understanding the facilitation of learning as a Christian and pastoral practice.

Conclusion

Organizations require both individual learning and organizational learning, so that reflection on the goals of the organization and the ways of meeting those goals (espoused theories and theories in use) can occur. Such reflection requires a willingness to engage in reflection on experience, and can deepen to different levels of reflection and learning (learning loops), from simple technical changes to more adaptive changes to changes concerning values and beliefs. Since individual learning is linked to organizational learning, organizations need to create various means of learning to accommodate different forms and depths of learning; such forms of learning ought to be relational and reflective. Complicated disorienting dilemmas provide opportunities for organizations to critically reflect on their beliefs in order to discern how faithful they are to their beliefs and how to improve their practices.

Management thus now requires facilitation of learning and reflection throughout the organization. The facilitator of learning then, in a sense, not only gives wise guidance in spreading knowledge but also assists in discerning the best path forward in an organization by gathering learning, giving it a hearing throughout the organization, and teaching skills necessary to make that learning fruitful in the organization.

In chapter 4, we will apply this concept of facilitation of learning to the role of the associate pastor, and suggest that the associate pastor can serve in the role of facilitator of learning in his or her organization.

CHAPTER 4

Associate Pastors as Facilitators of Learning

I f you've ever taken a tour of New York City, London, Venice, or Paris, you know that rivers bisect these famous cities; you have to cross a bridge that connects the two parts of the city and ties them together. In many cases the bridge itself is a prominent landmark: the Tower Bridge in London, the Rialto Bridge in Venice, and the Brooklyn Bridge in New York. The bridge is part of the tour; it provides connection to the two halves of the city.

Let's review the tour we've taken so far in this book. In the Introduction, we described associate pastors as managers working in ambiguous situations under the oversight of a senior pastor. We resolved to see if understanding associate pastors as facilitators of learning might help them embrace their roles as managers. In chapter 1, we developed a short theology of ministry, arguing that management is indeed a Spirit-empowered element of Christian ministry. In chapter 2 we described how organizations develop the complex relationships that make work ambiguous; and in chapter 3, we described how individual and organizational learning meet in the role of the facilitator of learning. While chapter 1 was largely scriptural, chapters 2 and 3 were heavy on organizational and educational theory. In this chapter we'll return to a theological orientation, as we integrate the facilitator-of-learning role with the role of the associate pastor.

This chapter is a bridge. It links the previous three chapters with the next three chapters, which will describe how associate pastors answered three overarching questions that pertain to being facilitators of learning: how they navigate complex relationships (chapter 5), how they facilitate their own learning (chapter 6), and how they facilitate their congregation's learning (chapter 7).

A Theological Review of Associate Pastoral Ministry

All pastors are called both by God and the church to preach, administer sacraments, and "guide and nurture the community towards full response to God's self-disclosure."[1] Therefore, stewarding the body of Christ in response to revelation and theology is critical to "cultivating a skilled and excellent life."[2] Recent scholarship has reemphasized the pastor as theologian, who facilitates theological learning in the local congregations.[3] In contrast, associate pastors are often seen as managers in their congregations.[4] Yet management, as we saw in chapter 2, is described with spiritual and theological language both by mainstream scholars and by the biblical text. Further, managers are also taking on new roles as coaches or facilitators of learning. Associate pastors are responsible for implementing the vision of leadership to the congregation, by connecting theology to the vision for all the congregational participants.

Volf and Croasmun suggest that the primary task of theology is to orient the church to a vibrant vision of human flourishing—the good life. In order to accomplish this task, theologians must align themselves with the vision and values of such a life, which requires their "reorientation and transformation. . . . It requires a death of the self and its rising and again and a resultant shift in seeing and hearing, *a new set of eyes and ears as the organs of the new self.*"[5] However,

---

1   Oden, *Pastoral Theology*, 50.
2   Charry, *By the Renewing of Your Minds*, 225.
3   Hiestand and Wilson, *The Pastor Theologian*, 80; cf. Vanhoozer, *The Pastor as Public Theologian*.
4   Boersma, "Managerial Competencies for Church Administration as Perceived by Seminary Faculties, Church Lay Leaders, and Ministers," 24; Radcliffe, *The Effective Ministry of an Associate Pastor*, 143–44.
5   Volf and Croasmun, *For the Life of the World*, 122, 124 (emphasis in original).

transformation is not a once-and-done event for theologians, nor indeed for any Christian.

> The initial revolution in orientation, the adoption of the new schema of the self and the world, is crucial, but it is just the beginning of a journey and of the process by which the self gets aligned with the new schema: "Keep being transformed," writes Paul [in Romans 12:2], using the present passive imperative.[6]

Since theologians are Christians in process as pilgrims to God's kingdom, [7] Volf and Croasmun suggest that theologians demonstrate an affinity for the good life they advocate through proleptic (imperfect) and ecstatic (outward) living; proleptic because such theologians can only strive imperfectly, and ecstatic because the good life lies outside of themselves and depends on God's work to achieve. "Theologians' lives, like the Christian life more generally, are not endeavors in self-achievement; their transformations are transformation of the self, but they are not mere *self*-transformations."[8] Since the life of a theologian is proleptic and ecstatic, so are their theological articulations,[9] which require that prayer and community frame their lives.[10] Theologians are "members of a collective body (1 Cor 12:27) that anticipates the eschatological unity of all in Christ (Gal 3:28)."[11] Theologians then both guide the church both in their proleptic and ecstatic lives and written articulations, which constantly require conversion and revision. But moreover, theologians are guided by the church, since the Spirit of God is "diffused through the church and possessed both imperfectly and communally."[12]

---

6   Volf and Croasmun, *For the Life of the World*, 124.
7   Volf and Croasmun, *For the Life of the World*, 128–29.
8   Volf and Croasmun, *For the Life of the World*, 130 (emphasis in original).
9   Volf and Croasmun, *For the Life of the World*, 131.
10 Volf and Croasmun, *For the Life of the World*, 134.
11 Volf and Croasmun, *For the Life of the World*, 134.
12 Volf and Croasmun, *For the Life of the World*, 134.

Pastors are theologians who not only must reorient their lives and their articulations to the truth of Jesus and the reality of the mission of the church, but must also guide their congregation's ministries proleptically and ecstatically while paying attention to what the Spirit is doing and saying in the life of their congregations. Associate pastors have the privilege of doing this task of theological and ministerial work from the center of their congregations.

Chapter 2 described pastors as shepherds, a metaphor Tidball takes up as the dominant paradigm for pastoral ministry: "This single image contains within it references to the authority, tender care, specific tasks, courage and sacrifice required of a pastor."[13] God models pastoral ministry as the shepherd who leads his people to provision and peace through danger (Ps. 23; cf. Ps. 28:9; 80:1). Israel's rulers were to shepherd like God, with integrity of heart and skilled hands (Ps. 78:2). Jesus fulfills this rule as the Good Shepherd who lays his life down for his sheep (John 10). The leaders of the church are meant to be under shepherds of Jesus (John 21:15–17, 1 Peter 2:25).

Shepherding presents ministry sometimes as pastor-centric and at other times as church-centric. On the one hand, shepherds (God, kings, or pastors) in the Bible protect, provide for, and guide the sheep: "Fundamentally, however, the task of shepherds is determined daily by the changing needs of the flock under their care."[14] Since the needs of a congregation can change daily, shepherding or pastoring requires the management of not only resources but of ambiguity itself.[15] On the other hand, Willimon uses the image of manager to describe pastors as leaders of an incarnational faith, and sees management as a positive way of empowering congregants rather than doing ministry for the congregants.[16] This aligns with the understanding of "pastor" and "elder" in Scripture. While elders and pastors must be apt to teach, they must also be good relationship and resource man-

13   Tidball, *Skilful Shepherds*, 54.
14   Laniak, *Shepherds after My Own Heart*, 247.
15   Tsui, et al., "Dealing with Discrepant Expectations," 1515.
16   Willimon, *Pastor*, 61–62.

agers of their households (1 Tim. 3:2, Titus 1:6; 2:1). The teaching ministry of the church leaders therefore facilitates the agency of the whole congregation to good deeds and maturity (Eph. 4:11–16, cf. 1 Cor. 12:7–11). Willimon writes, "As we have said, the pastor is the 'community person,' the one who is ordained by the church to worry about internal congregational concerns. So the issue is not, 'Should I be concerned with internal administration?' but rather, 'How should I be concerned with administration?'"[17]

An apt descriptor for pastor and shepherd might be a steward who manages both resources and people in order to reach the organization's goals.[18] Wilson develops a biblical theology metaphor for leadership rooted in God's ownership of creation (Lev. 25:23–28; Deut. 8:17; 10:14; Ps. 24:1) and the creation mandate given to humanity (Gen. 1:26–27).[19] While writing for faith-based nonprofits, Wilson's definition of steward leadership is transferable to pastors and churches: "Steward leadership is the efficient management and growth of organizational resources, through leadership of staff and activities as a non-owning steward-servant, in order to achieve the mission according to the owners."[20]

Management, understood through the lens of facilitating learning, is then a critical pastoral task that incorporates shepherding congregants in direction God is leading; it requires theological reflection on living, thus stewarding the congregants themselves and their gifts to accomplish the tasks God has given to their congregation.

Who's Facilitating Whom?

Who and what exactly is an associate pastor facilitating when he or she acts as a facilitator of learning? This section outlines how associate pastors may facilitate their learning and the congregation's learning, as well as facilitate the congregation's ministries.

---

17   Willimon, *Pastor*, 62.
18   Wilson, *Steward Leadership in the Nonprofit Organization*, 6, 86.
19   Wilson, *Steward Leadership in the Nonprofit Organization*, 51–52.
20   Wilson, *Steward Leadership in the Nonprofit Organization*, 86. In this case, as Wilson points out, the owner of the church is God.

Associate Pastors Facilitate Their Own Individual Learning

Timothy is advised to watch the interaction of his own life and doctrine closely (1 Tim. 4:16). The merger of life and doctrine depends on linking practice to scriptural revelation (James 1:22–25, 2:8) and doctrinal faith (James 2:14–19). The merger of life and doctrine requires wisdom (James 3:13–17), which is a gift generously given by God (James 1:5, 17) and is best expressed as loving one's neighbor (James 2:8).

Associate Pastors Facilitate Their Own Congregation's Organizational Learning

Integration of life and doctrine is a critical concern for both pastors and congregations, hence Paul's urgency to appoint elders in Crete (Titus 1:4). Paul urges sacrificial living as a response to God's mercy (Rom. 12:1), achieved through renewed minds used to discern God's will (Rom. 12:2). The transformational process is communal; all believers are to renew their minds while offering themselves by exercising spiritual gifts (12:6–8), which generates sincere love for one another (12:9) and fulfills God's word and law (13:9–10).

Tidball saw pastoral theology as "the interface between theology and Christian doctrine on the one hand, and pastoral experience and care on the other. As such, it is found to be a discipline in tension. It is not a theology in the abstract, but theology seen from the shepherding perspective."[21] While Tidball normally saw theology as more fundamentally and necessarily informing shepherding perspectives, he also cautiously allowed that shepherding could inform theology. Branson and Martínez utilize a reflective approach, or praxis, to pastoral theology which they describe as "a continual movement from experience to reflection and to study, and then on to new actions and experience."[22] They write further:

---

21 Tidball, *Skilful Shepherds*, 24.
22 Branson and Martínez, *Churches, Cultures, and Leadership*, 40–41.

So in a church, praxis is the constant rhythm that includes study and reflection (including works of theology and other theoretical material) in continual interaction with engagement and action. A church's capacity to discern and participate in God's will is increased whenever this rhythm is well resourced and intentional.[23]

Since theology is properly grounded in Scripture, it is possible to develop a set of learning loops that inform theory (or in this case, theology) and practice that develop an interaction between revelation and beliefs (study) and values and action (practice). These learning loops are described in Figure 4-1. These learning loops apply to the associate pastor in particular but are also applicable to the church congregation as a whole.

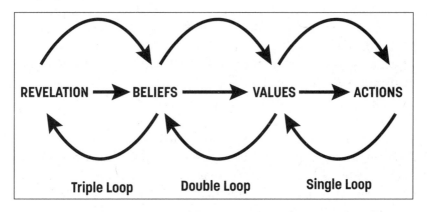

Figure 4-1: Associate Pastor and Congregational Learning Loops

Associate pastors must facilitate growth in the congregation by engaging the diverse mental models of congregational members through organizational learning.[24] Associate pastors have to be competent to

---

23   Branson and Martínez, *Churches, Cultures, and Leadership*, 41–42.

24   Kim, "The Link between Individual and Organizational Learning"; Senge, *The Fifth Discipline*; Ellinger, "Antecedents and Consequences of Coaching Behavior."

understand their own mental models through an orthodox theological lens and work to help their congregations understand their own mental models of the world, since mental models are perspectival.[25] The associate pastor must be thoughtful in taking diverse mental models and allowing their unique perspectives to complement one another and develop the congregation, as long as they are done in accordance with God's Word.

Associate Pastors Facilitate Their Congregation's Ministries

Associate pastors are also described as implementers of their congregations' ministries. As such, they often face the brunt of ambiguity and the challenges it produces. By employing a facilitator-of-learning role, associate pastors may be able to discern, with the congregation, more fruitful possibilities for growth in the congregation in order to direct the congregation's specific ministries.

This may be possible through at least two learning disciplines: repentance and discernment. I will briefly describe them here, and return to them at the end of chapter 8.

Repentance

The discipline of repentance is rooted in the gospel. Jesus preached, "Repent, for the kingdom of heaven is near" (Matt. 4:17). Repentance is not simply acknowledging past mistakes and confessing sin, but reorienting to a new way of life made possible by Jesus's death and resurrection and the outpouring of the Holy Spirit on the church (Acts 1:37–39; Rom. 3:21; Gal. 2:20–21; Eph. 1). Consequently, repentance has both a past and future dimension, as congregations pursue God's will. Repentance is also a corporate endeavor; the refusal to conform to the pattern of the world but to be transformed by the renewing of our mind is a plural work of the entire church as it seeks to renew its common mind to the pattern of Jesus Christ (Rom. 12:1–2).[26]

---

25   Senge, *The Fifth Discipline*, 164.
26   Van Gelder, *The Ministry of the Missional Church*, 115.

When put alongside Mezirow's theory of transformation, one can see that repentance requires a robust imagination to see the world through a new way of being in the world, through changing perspective both on one's self and their setting; such work is at once individual and corporate[27] and requires support and dialogue.[28] Elmer and Elmer thus emphasize the church as a community of priests who support one another in growth and spiritual maturity:[29]

> When New Testament priests [that is, Christians] exercise their spiritual gifts, they are connecting with and nurturing one another—each giving and each receiving. Secularists may call this "social discourse" but Christians call this "ministry"—the ministry of being Christ to one another.[30]

They further suggest that learning through role-playing, building accountability relationships, managing social pressures, avoiding dangerous contexts, managing negative thoughts, and depending on Scripture and prayer are good ways to facilitate behavior change so that repentance is possible.[31]

Discernment

The discernment paradigm is "the capacity to recognize and respond to the presence and activity of God."[32] Like the repentance paradigm, discernment is also rooted in the gospel. Jesus promises the gift of the Holy Spirit to the disciples, who will guide them into all truth (John 16:3) and remind them of what he taught (John 14:26). The Holy Spirit provides a common bond between the gospel and the church (Eph. 1:13–14; 4:4–6) and gives believers the mind of Christ (1 Cor. 2:10–16). Through the Holy Spirit's work, believers

---

27   Mezirow, "Learning to Think Like an Adult," 8.
28   Mezirow, "Learning to Think Like an Adult," 25; Elmer and Elmer, *The Learning Cycle*, 140–41.
29   Elmer and Elmer, *The Learning Cycle*, 142–43.
30   Elmer and Elmer, *The Learning Cycle*, 143.
31   Elmer and Elmer, *The Learning Cycle*, 120–24.
32   Barton, *Pursuing God's Will Together*, 10.

may discern God's by setting their mind on the Spirit (Rom. 8:5). Discernment connects to repentance: As believers respond to God's mercy, they offer themselves completely to God as a living sacrifice, by not conforming to the pattern of the world but by being transformed through the renewal of the mind, so they may discern God's perfect will (Rom. 12:1–20).

Discernment has both an individual and corporate aspect and is practiced through the guidance of a facilitator.[33] Discernment has elements of discourse[34] and dialogue.[35]

Discernment requires discourse, which "is dialogue involving the assessment of beliefs, feelings and values."[36] Discourse requires emotional maturity among its participants.[37] In addition, Cranton and Mezirow suggest that discourse requires access to information, freedom from both coercion and personal blindness, the ability to judge evidence and critique presuppositions, and the ability to accept consensus decisions.[38] As such, discourse is collaborative thinking, which is distinct from "argument culture," which frames discussion as winning and losing.[39] Discourse is essential to critical thinking, since it is a social learning process best done in small groups.[40]

Isaacs suggests that negotiation and dialogue differ from one another:

> The aim of negotiation is to reach agreement among parties who differ. The intention of dialogue is to reach new understanding and, in doing so, to form a totally new basis from which to think and act. In dialogue, one not only

---

33   Barton, *Pursuing God's Will Together*, 11, 178.
34   Mezirow, "Learning to Think Like an Adult"; Cranton, *Understanding and Promoting Transformative Learning*.
35   Isaac, *Dialogue and the Art of Thinking Together*; Bohm, *On Dialogue*.
36   Cranton, *Understanding and Promoting Transformative Learning*, 24.
37   Mezirow, "Learning to Think Like an Adult," 11.
38   Cranton, *Understanding and Promoting Transformative Learning*, 24; Mezirow, "Learning to Think Like an Adult," 12.
39   Mezirow, "Learning to Think Like an Adult," 11.
40   Brookfield, *Teaching for Critical Thinking*, 55.

solves problems, one dissolves them. We do not merely try to reach agreement, we try to create a context from which many new contexts can come.[41]

As such, negotiation might be thought of as a first-loop type of learning. Negotiators attempt to solve technical or instrumental problems. Negotiation arises from a defense of a position. It is analytic and "uses hard data to answers problems."[42] Nonetheless, Fisher, Ury, and Patton recognize that negotiation is still relational: "Any method of negotiation may be fairly judged by three criteria: It should produce a wise agreement if agreement is possible. It should be efficient. And it should improve or at least not damage the relationship between the parties."[43] But dialogue is a second learning loop, where one changes the context to rethink the possibilities of an organization. Similar to discourse, dialogue requires a suspension of judgment (as opposed to a defense of position) in order to reflect on assumptions.[44] "Reflective dialogue can then give rise to generative dialogue, in which we begin to create entirely new possibilities and create levels of interaction."[45]

"Discernment is an ever-increasing capacity to 'see' or discern the works of God in the midst of the human situation so that we can align ourselves with whatever it is that God is doing."[46] Discernment is communal, contextual, as leaders together seek God's will in order to make decisions.[47] Discernment steps beyond mere human conversation to ask "What is God doing in this situation, and how can I get on board with it?"[48] Like critical reflection, discernment works to alleviate blindness caused by existing paradigms.

---

41 Isaacs, *Dialogue and the Art of Thinking Together,* 19.
42 Isaacs, *Dialogue and the Art of Thinking Together,* 41.
43 Fisher, Ury, and Patton, *Getting to Yes,* 40.
44 Isaacs, *Dialogue and the Art of Thinking Together,* 41.
45 Isaacs, *Dialogue and the Art of Thinking Together,* 38.
46 Barton, *Pursuing God's Will Together,* 20.
47 Barton, *Pursuing God's Will Together,* 20.
48 Barton, *Pursuing God's Will Together,* 22.

Conclusion

In this chapter, I've argued that associate pastors attempt to integrate theology with the practices and ministries of their congregations. As such, associate pastors are indeed pastor-theologians, but their theology is about living proleptically and ecstatically toward a vision of the good life—a vision which must be shared and taught to the congregation. Thus, associate pastors are also shepherds who provide guidance and structure for the living of that vision in their congregations as managers. Therefore, the facilitator-of-learning paradigm is a helpful guide for the associate pastor role. Associate pastors facilitate their own learning and the learning of the congregation in addition to the congregation's ministries. They can do this by employing reflective discourse, dialogue, and discernment with congregational members.

The next three chapters describe how associate pastors described themselves in terms of their congregational complexity, their own learning, and the learning of others. The final chapter will describe six major skills that will help associate pastors as facilitators of learning.

CHAPTER 5

Pinched Associate Pastors

Ever play the childhood game "monkey-in-the-middle"? I played this game with older and taller relatives at family reunions when I was growing up. It was a fun but frustrating game because I wasn't tall or fast enough to stay out of the middle; I simply couldn't catch the ball. And even if I did catch it, one of the taller adults in the middle would recover it, and I would end up in the middle again.

However, when I played soccer as a young boy, I really enjoyed playing in the midfield. Midfielders are responsible for viewing the whole field and moving the ball from the defenders to the forwards, who attack the opposite goal. Midfielders aren't supposed to leave the middle of the field; they allow the forwards to score goals and the defense to protect the backfield. But in and from the middle, midfielders can change the dynamic of the game with a well-timed kick to a player in the right position either in front of or behind them. The midfield yields a place of power.

In the same way, the middle yields both frustrations and possibilities for associate pastors. The following three chapters will describe how twenty-five different associate pastors understood their ministry from the middle of the congregation. Remember, these twenty-five pastors represented a wide variety of denominational backgrounds, had different job descriptions, and included both male and female and ethnically diverse associate pastors. The model that follows represents how they understand associate ministry and how they ministered as facilitators of learning.

Before we learn how associate pastors minister from the middle, we have to learn how their congregations are set up. What do congregations and middleness look like to associate pastors? Therefore, this particular chapter will examine how the "field" of the congregation is set up for the associate pastor by answering the question: "How do associate pastors navigate complexity in their congregational systems?"

The next chapter will describe how associate pastors, in view of their responsibilities and roles, facilitate their own learning so they can perform their duties well. The third chapter will then describe how associate pastors facilitate the learning of the remainder of the congregation.

As a brief note, I will abbreviate associate pastor as AP and senior pastor as SP going forward in the next three chapters.

What Do We Mean by Complexity?

One of my friends is a little league soccer coach. He took the job simply so his son could burn off steam and get exercise with friends. While he had a simple goal (let every child on the team play and have fun) he was confronted by the other parents' goal (let the best kids play so the team could win). Of course, my friend had to expend energy and time negotiating with parents and children about who would play and why. It was, to say the least, complicated.

Complexity is an organizational term that describes how multiple streams of information, different relationships with organizational constituencies, and changing environmental factors make decision-making and action complicated in a particular system. Congregations are organizational systems, just as families, companies, governments, and nonprofits are. They are therefore subject to complexity. Christians sometimes bemoan such complexity as a result of the fallen human condition, and certainly sin further deepens complexity in any organization. But any time people are gathered together into a specific organizational structure, whatever that structure is (or, in the case of churches, whatever the polity of the specific denomination is), complexity naturally arises because that is how organizations and cultures work. The problem is not to eliminate complexity, but to learn to navigate it as a Christian and as a pastor—specifically, in the case of our study, as an associate pastor.

How Do Associate Pastors Navigate Complexity in Their Congregational Systems?

Like a spider sitting at the center of a complicated web, the associate pastors (APs) we spoke to found themselves at the center of a complex web of interactions that systemically impacted how they facilitated learning.

APs navigate their congregational systems in four primary ways. First, they try to establish mutual trust with their senior pastors (SPs). Second, they work through complicated relationships with their governing boards. Third, they experience camaraderie with other APs or ministry staff in the middle. Fourth and finally, they work through complicated relationships with key leaders in their congregations.

Associate Pastors Work to Establish Mutual Trust with Their Senior Pastors

When married couples take their vows, they both recite and receive the same promises and obligations. The vows are not the burden of the bride only, nor are they the burden of the groom only. Rather, they are reciprocal; both husband and wife give themselves in trust to the other and expect that gift to be returned. Such vows emphasize the significance of mutual trust in marriage, and indeed in all human relationships, though the promises and obligations are different.

As seen previously, research already describes how SPs influence their APs. So it is no surprise that the APs in this study also emphasized this relationship as the presence or lack of mutual trust. Such trust is a reciprocal confidence and respect defined by open and honest relationships, and by the freedom to accomplish clearly understood pastoral responsibilities. Even though these relationships were often complicated and asymmetrical, APs either trusted or wanted to trust their SPs. At the same time, they desired to have their SPs trust in their pastoral work.

Developing Trust with Senior Pastors

Associate pastors developed trust with their senior pastors in three pivotal ways. They built relationships, they kept clear communication lines open (about their own ministries and conditions in the congregation), and they supported their SP's vision and decisions.

Building Relationships with Senior Pastors

Time helps in building relationships and trust. In the interviews, APs expressed high levels of support for their SPs; many had long tenures in their congregations under a single pastor. Alex, Micah, Paul, and Sam had only ever served a single SP. Logan had been with his SP for ten years: "So he's been here for twelve years. I know him like a book now." Likewise, Paul served twenty years with a single SP, and the time together allowed them to build trust. "In the highs and lows of life, I could go to him, and he would pray for me, encourage me, and give me good wisdom." APs also appreciated their SP's longevity at their congregations; Micah (an African American) stated his deep indebtedness to his white SP for staying in a difficult community for more than thirty years.

> We've been friends for a very long time. And so my relationship with him is a deep friend. I'm so indebted to him, because of his commitment to hanging in the community, during the height of racial tension at the time. For him to come and live here and walk with him through many of his struggles with people in our neighborhood, because he's white.

APs who served multiple SPs also expressed trust and loyalty to them. In these situations, the AP served as the consistent pastoral presence in the church. As a case in point, Kathy described her role in her church as "continuity":

> I've been here nine years; this is the third senior pastor I've worked with. So, in my review last year, they said I'm the glue that's held the congregation together. And that's one of my

gifts. It's the relationships, I'm grounded. I'm just here. And for this congregation, that's what the associate role means.

Yet she developed a trusting relationship with each SP, though each one had a different role in her life. The first SP she described as a father, the second as a mentor, and the third as a peer partnership, yet each had her loyalty.

In all three cases, Kathy had caring SPs who served as friends. Not all APs had warm relationships with their SPs, but the professional relationships worked as long as reciprocating trust was present. For example, Alex described his SP as "warm enough," but did not label him a close friend. Erin reported a similar feeling; she never was a "Starbucks buddy" with her SP. Likewise, Henry worked well with his previous SP but never sensed that his SP cared about him or his family; in all the time they served together they were never invited into his SP's home: "We never really even had a meal together."

Since trust meant loyalty, APs noted that if an AP could no longer support their SP, the AP should leave the congregation. Erin, for example, stated, "The minute that you cannot be supportive of your SP, you better get a different job." Likewise, Eric said, "I've been taught this since I was younger, and I believe it. There is one leader, one key top leader of the church. And loyalty is essential." Later in the interview, he stated: "You know, the church doesn't need you to create division, to go against your SP. If you are there and you discover [reasons to leave], you quietly find God's call somewhere else." However, APs also feared being let go if they didn't support their SPs. Describing a hyper-driven SP, Carol said: "If you didn't run at [his] pace, you might as well go." Kathy, speaking about a SP with whom she had a good relationship, stated frankly: "If we weren't doing well, I would be out. And I know it. That's just how it would be."

Keeping Communication Channels Open with Senior Pastors

APs also demonstrated trust in their SPs by keeping clear channels of communication. APs did not want their SPs to be surprised by activities, programming, or decisions being made. Erin, from years of serving, knew exactly what information she needed to pass along to her SPs in order to keep their trust and confidence, yet without overwhelming them with details:

> You know, it's like I am totally trusted; again, I've done this a long time. I know what people want to know, I know what the senior pastor wants to know, I've just done this a long time. So, I make sure I inform them. "Just want you to know, so-and-so's under hospice care. In my opinion, this person probably has three weeks in this world, more or less." So I inform them. I'm very good about that.

Alex described open communication as a way of displaying loyalty and organizational stability. He told his SP that he would never be blindsided by coups in the church or by decisions in his ministry.

> When he was hired, I told him, "So far as it depends on me, you're never going to be blindsided. If there is a problem in my ministry, you will hear about it from me first. If there's a coup that's about to be thrown, I'm not going to let you be surprised by that."

Supporting the Senior Pastor's Vision and Decisions

APs worked to support their SP's vision in front of the congregation. This support was often expressed as the implementation of the SP's organizational vision for the congregation. Becca defined her relationship with her SP as leaning into his vision and his direction. Diana, who was older than her SP, supported his vision by becoming a liaison to the senior adults of her congregation. Likewise, Alex described his support for his SP as a willingness to support and implement decisions that were made. "I might disagree with a decision made, but once a decision is made, it's time for me to line up." Eric emphatically believed that the SP's decisions needed to be abided by the APs on staff: "If the answer is no, it's no."

Desiring Trust from Senior Pastors

Ever have friends who were always expected to travel home to visit their relatives? They might complain, "Why don't they come here more often? After all, the road runs two ways!" This sentiment expresses how APs feel about their senior pastors. As seen above, APs learned to develop relationships with their SP, keep communication open with their SP, and support their SP's vision and decisions. But APs also needed to receive and experience trust from their SPs to perform their roles. Ministry requires that the relationship between APs and SPs be a two-way street, not a one-way street.

What would a two-way relationship with SPs look like? APs expressed three significant expressions of trust from their SPs in order to perform their roles within their organizations: access to their SPs, appropriate accountability, and freedom to perform their pastoral duties creatively.

Access to Senior Pastors

APs expressed a need for access to their SPs in order to stay synchronized with vision and expectations. Farrah felt she and her fellow staff had outstanding access to their SP, which she felt was not the case amongst some of her peers in other churches: "We can go in and chat with him anytime." Access to the SP is not simply giving reports, but the ability to dialogue and come to consensus through intentional conversation. Diana likewise felt that she could go to her SP at any time and seek clarity.

Access could be spiritual as well as informational. SPs could take postures of spiritual openness to their APs. For example, Brad described his access and conversations with his SP as "very open and very honest." He went further: "They usually involve prayer. He is really good at asking questions, and getting me to unpack certain things, and process things, so they help me to process things, what I'm doing."

APs also appreciated their SP's ability to receive criticism and to work things out behind closed doors. Alex, who often acted as a devil's advocate, appreciated his SP's willingness to engage his probes.

Likewise, Sam described the SP-to-AP relationship in his church as "He's the gas man, and I'm the brake man." Frank and his SP had a "tell it like it is" policy that made their partnership particularly effective. Brad felt he had the freedom to deeply influence the preaching schedule of the church, but noted that his SP could get annoyed if he pushed back too much.

Not having access to their SPs was problematic for APs. For example, Amy shared that her fellow APs were jealous that they could not get face time with their SP because he was often off-site, mentoring pastors in other churches: "That's hurtful to them." Similarly, Isaac put his own lack of access to his SP this way: "It hurt the relationship the first five years in the ministry, because I was struggling with certain issues on leadership teams that were difficult for me to deal with, and could have used his help and he's just not that available to us, because he's got so much going on."

Appropriate Accountability

Sometimes APs had to work very hard to clarify expectations with their SPs, but the payoff was security in knowing they were on task. Logan communicated extensively with his SP to keep in step with him, "because we need to be on the same page." Paul stated that he thrived in an environment where there was high autonomy and high accountability. "I want to know that I'm doing right; I want to know that I am hitting the target, the bull's eye." Colin, in describing a lackluster relationship with his former SP, noted that the relationship worked with the right amount of accountability and freedom. "As long as the youth ministry was going fine, he was kind of hands-off." Alex appreciated the reciprocation of trust from his SP: "We're allowed to have disagreements, but I need to know he's not going to throw me under the bus, in front of the elders for example, and I don't think that he will."

Freedom to Be Creative

While APs strived to stay connected to their congregation's framework and their SPs' expectations, they also wanted to be allowed the freedom necessary to perform their tasks creatively. Alex felt that his freedom was tied to the trust he developed with his SP: "He's given me a lot of slack on the leash to lead." Becca felt she had room to be creative because her congregation was willing to take risks, "And what that tells me: they bring with them a spirit of willingness to try new things. They don't worry too much about failure or risk in the process." On the more negative side, Brad felt he didn't have the permission he needed to execute his vision for evangelism and one-on-one discipleship: "When you say 'make a disciple,' for the last three years I have wanted to do something at this church, but I have not felt the freedom to do it—and not just from the leaders, but from the adults too."

APs particularly desired freedom from micromanagement; they didn't like feeling as if someone was looking over their shoulder, telling them exactly what to do or giving nagging feedback. Henry stated about his multiple SP relationships, "When I've had in the past were SPs that were more hands-on and telling me what I needed to do and giving me a lot of criticism. That's actually where I struggled a lot, and I had a lot of difficulty, to be able to have the freedom to do the ministry that God has enabled me to do."

Tensions in Senior Pastor and Associate Pastor Relationships

All relationships carry some amount of anxiety and tension; AP and SP relationships are clearly no exception. We've already seen some APs note that their SPs don't like too much pushback. APs experienced a relational tension with SPs when they attempted to negotiate the multiple roles of partner, mentor, and friend. Earlier in the chapter Kathy described her successive SPs as father, mentor, and peer/partner, respectively. Likewise, John described his first SP as a father, and the second as a brother. Yet, the SP and AP need not be close friends in order to navigate the church well. You may remember that Alex described his relationship with his SP as "warm enough." However, other APs longed for deeper friendship with their SPs. Colin, in particular, was greatly relieved when a more relationally distant SP was followed by another SP who was warmer, and who openly invited his family into his home:

> [The new pastor] is kind of a big and, in my opinion, welcome change. He's much more of a pastor's pastor. He's very understanding toward other pastoral families and what we go through. He is just very supportive.

APs sometimes express frustration at being limited by the asymmetrical dynamic between them and their SPs. Both APs are SPs are often highly educated, ordained to ministry, and good friends. These dynamics are symmetric. Yet the dimension of overseer and subordinate creates an imposing asymmetry to the relationship. Frank, for example, felt both relieved and limited that the buck stopped with the SP and not with him. However, Owen felt frustrated by his SP's inability to be team-oriented, cut bureaucratic red tape, and move boundaries. Becca described the asymmetry of the relationship by contrasting the subordinate nature of her role with equal education and credentials she and her SP possessed: "I call him my boss all the time, and he's like, 'Don't call me that.' And I'm like, 'Well I need to; for my sake, I need to.'"

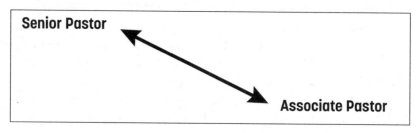

Figure 5-1: Senior Pastor and Associate Pastor Relationship

Figure 5-1 describes the asymmetrical relationship of the SP and the AP. While in a subordinate role, APs and SPs must navigate multiple tensions of trust and responsibility in their relationships to work well together in their congregations. But other relationships also influence APs and their work, including their relationships with their governing boards.

Associate Pastors Have Complicated Relationships with Their Governing Boards

In college I served on a volunteer crew at a Habitat for Humanity, with a group of retired builders. They perpetually argued with each other and the head contractor about details, from where to lay the floor joists to the type of nail being used. As the new volunteer on site, I was told by several people to do different things on the same project at the same time. Who should I listen to?

This is what it often feels for associate pastors when it comes to their relationships with the governing boards of their church. While denominations have different traditions concerning church government, many congregations have a board that oversees the church's ministry. This board is composed of a variety of people with different interests and values. As might be expected, the AP's relationship with these individual board members are complex and complicated.

Depending on experience, ordination, or other factors, APs might be on the board either as a full participant, a partial participant, or not at all. APs were sometimes given formalized roles on the elder board or the controlling board of their church. When this arrangement happens, APs are usually recognized as pastors by their elders or governing board members. Often they participate on their church's boards, though sometimes not as elders.

Sam was a nonvoting elder with a number of other APs at his church, but they rotated on and off the board so as not to overpower the lay elders. Frank, on the other hand, was not an elder but felt his pastoral position gave him some voice at the elder meetings: "It definitely came and comes with authority. I'm not an elder, but I do sit in on the elder meetings. And I can voice my opinion freely. But I don't get to vote on anything as they are choosing to decide what to do."

However, even when they were given formal board roles, APs had to balance board responsibilities with their competing positions of being subordinate to the SP (cf. Figure 5-2). For example Sam, while sitting on the board, found himself in an unexpected theological disagreement with his SP. Such complications can exist even if the AP is not an elder. Frank and his SP had a cordial disagreement about whether or not a vision statement was too long, and had the elders decide between the two perspectives. Logan put it succinctly: "It's awkward because, as an AP, I serve under [my SP]. As an elder I'm his equal. And so, that's an awkward place to be just because that's two different roles."

Other APs, while not on their churches' governing boards, had relationships of influence with their board members, wherein they influenced the direction of the top leaders of the church. Such influence takes place through a variety of interactions. Erin, tasked with pastoral care, would "wine and dine" board members in order to present pressing care needs that required extra financial assistance. Alex negotiated a change in his job description with his SP, executive pastor, and the chairman of the board. He had to defend decisions made to terminate three small groups causing dissension in the church to the elder board, even though he had the authority to do it. Isaac had to negotiate the end of a burdensome children's volunteer dinner that volunteers didn't attend. The elders were initially unwilling to let the event die, but Isaac slowly negotiated small changes to the event until the elders saw that it was unnecessary.

Negotiations do not always go in the AP's favor. Brad was asked by his SP for ideas for an upcoming sermon series. After coming up with a series of suggestions, the elder board met with the SP during a retreat and suggested different topics, which the SP chose over his AP's ideas.

In board interactions, APs can find allies in particular board members who will listen to them in ways the SP doesn't. For example, Reese stated, "When I'm sitting down with the chairman of the elder board, then I feel like I represent the church. I can speak on behalf of the church. I can talk about what I would like to see in the church."

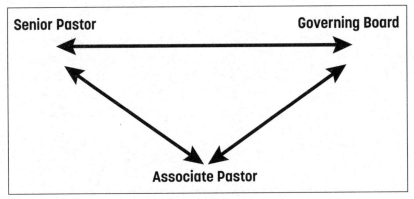

**Figure 5-2: Senior Pastor, Board,
and Associate Pastor Relationships**

Navigating Tensions Between Board Members and the Congregation

On occasion, SPs might be caught in tensions between the governing board of the church and the congregation at large. For example, some APs who were given the right to vote on their governing boards refused to do so because they faced the tension of being an elder and a pastor of the congregation. Diana did not want to be the board member who might cast the deciding vote. She strongly felt that her abstention from voting kept her in good relationship with the whole congregation.

> The problem is, if you vote, what if the motion wins by one vote? So you are on the deciding end of a decision. My feeling always is that you have to work in such a way where you can be candid about where you stand, but you have to stay in relationship with everybody in the church. So to be a deciding vote, I would never want that role. So I choose not to vote.

In another example, Irene described a very jarring situation in which the elder board had to defend a specific decision to the congregation. The APs took a posture of keeping doors open to congregants and listening to their concerns, but had to balance that with supporting their church's and denomination's stance. John described another tension between board members and church members regarding whether or not the church ought to revise their philosophy of ministry. The board itself was divided on the issue and was experiencing with the congregation something that John described as "vision collision." The AP tension between the elder board and the congregation is depicted in Figure 5-3.

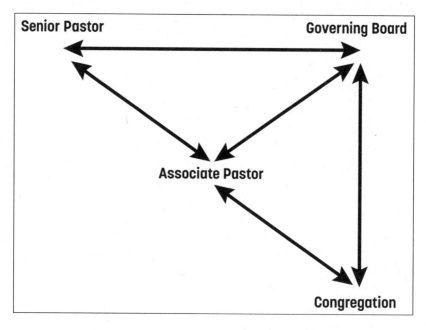

Figure 5-3: Senior Pastor, Board, Congregation, and Associate Pastor Relationships

Associate Pastors Experience Camaraderie with Other Mid-Level Staff

While most APs reported warm relationships with their SPs, APs at churches with other APs and ministerial staff usually described highly collaborative friendships among their parallel colleagues. Isaac described his mid-level relationships as supportive and fun: "It's like going to work with your high school friends." David, at a different church, described a similar relationship with his colleagues: "I call us the three musketeers! The worship leader, the youth pastor, myself. We really work close together!"

Alex discussed intentional collaborative interaction with the children's ministry director, particularly over curriculum selection and sharing volunteers. Their relationship worked well in part because they were willing to surrender their "sacred cows" for the good of the church. Brad noted that the mid-level staff served in each other's ministries. Farrah told a similar story: "We are good friends. We figure out together where the church needs to go. We are very close, with hardly any sense of being in our own silos."

Some APs had a mentoring role at the mid-level. For example, Amy took a mentoring role toward other APs in her church, taking responsibility for their spiritual formation and job training: "The other associates, the ones that we have now, I trained them all."

APs could also experience stressful mid-level staff relationships. For example, Colin's church hired a former SP into an AP role. This new hire had trouble staying in the boundaries of his role and often acted like a SP toward the existing pastors. Colin and his fellow associates felt as if they were being demeaned by the new hire, and the actual SP had to correct the behavior. Noah faced a challenge with other associate pastors jockeying for revised job descriptions. Noah also shared that female staff felt as if the male staffers had an all-boys club amongst themselves.

Meanwhile, Jenna experienced a strain in relationships at the mid-level when her SP went on vacation or was out of town. A friend on staff struggled to relate to Jenna as an authority, making for awkward tensions: "So, I feel like what I have to do is actually step back a little bit from the friendship, which is not my first choice, because you know, what am I going to do? Quit my job?"

Siloing[1] did occur in some AP ministries. Noah didn't mind silos and felt that his area of ministry didn't need input from other APs.

---

1   Siloing is a phenomenon where different ministries within a church are tacitly or explicitly separated from one another, with no collaborative interaction or integration to other ministries.

On the other hand, Greg felt that the APs in his church fit too well into their niches and didn't have any overlap or connection through a common vision.

Loneliness could be a result of silos for APs, or when they were the only AP on staff. Mark relished seminary because there was more social interaction: "It also was helpful just to get out of the church day-to-day, because it's lonely being in ministry all the time." Kathy described the relationship as being isolated as she navigated the relationship with the SP. "There is no one else who does my job. . . . I've thought about it often, that it would be fun to have another associate. What would it be like to work at a two-associate church? To have somebody who is really on the same playing field? Because being an associate is hard."

Associate Pastors Have Complicated Relationships with Key Leaders

Earlier I mentioned that I worked a summer as a construction worker for Habitat for Humanity. Before the weekend, regular volunteers would set up work projects for weekend volunteers. Some of these teams were fantastic; they were skilled, responsible, and eager. Other teams were eager but not nearly as skilled. After the weekend, regular volunteers would visit the work projects to fix problems weekend volunteers had caused. The regulars would say to themselves, "The strength of Habitat is its volunteers. And the weakness of Habitat is its volunteers."

As we've seen, APs have complex and complicated relationships with SPs, governing boards, and their comrades at the mid-level. This dynamic occurs at the top of the congregational organization, but a very similar dynamic exists with key leaders and volunteers who serve in the APs' ministries. And like the relationships with SPs, several of the APs interviewed described very complicated relationships with the key leaders of their congregations. APs had an array of relationships in the congregations that were both positive and negative. While it might be tempting to suggest that the strength of APs' ministry are their volunteers and the weakness of APs' ministries are their volunteers, it would be closer to the truth to say, "The strength of APs' ministries are their *relationships* with their volunteers, and the weakness of APs' ministries are their *relationships* with their volunteers." Fostering productive relationships with key volunteers was essential to their ministries.

Four particular challenges face APs when working with key leaders. First, APs often partner with high-capacity volunteers. Second, they can sometimes face uncooperative volunteers. Third, key leaders have mixed perceptions of APs. And finally, associate pastors must reciprocate trust with key leaders.

Partnering with High-Capacity Volunteers

APs often work with high-capacity leaders—highly successful and impactful professionals from a variety of fields. For example, churches near seminaries often had highly educated professors. One church's population was made up of state employees and health care workers; another church was composed primarily of engineers and professional managers. Farrah thought such congregants created higher levels of expectation in churches in terms of presentation and ministry programming. Becca agreed: "I have people who are very comfortable financially, and that means that they have high expectations about the kind of things that we roll out and the kind of systems that we have." David suggested that high-capacity volunteers needed a facilitative form of leadership other than direct command-and-control.

A challenge that APs face with high-capacity volunteers is their critique of the AP's performance. Sam, previous to his ministry role, was a high-capacity volunteer and remembers critiquing the AP who preceded him: "I had to full-on repent to him." Paul was frustrated by high-capacity people critiquing his ministry: "This is such an interesting dynamic because you have people, whatever their field of work is, who feel like they are an expert in your field." He painted an imaginary scene where he went into a volunteer's business to critique his management, and what his volunteer would say. "It's absurd. 'Who do you think you are?' Yet, when they turn around and do it to us pastors, well it's a whole differently matter entirely."

Facing Uncooperative Leaders

APs occasionally ran into difficult challenges in fostering participation with key leaders in the congregation. Noah had a high-capacity volunteer who refused to follow the vision of the ministry: "He came to me and said, 'I know what you are trying to get us to do. And we are not going to do it.'" Frank experienced a similar problem in his small group ministry's focusing on sermon studies when he hoped to have his small groups be more evangelistic. "We've had some pushback," he said succinctly, as he struggled to get some volunteers to leadership meetings. Brad struggled to motivate volunteers to take larger steps toward leading ministries or projects, due to a deep respect but overdependence on pastoral leadership. Sam felt challenged and manipulated by a volunteer who pushed him to start a worship band. Henry struggled to get some of his adult leaders to fully commit to the programming and develop deep relationships, and was frustrated when adult volunteers exhibited more investment in serving when they became deacons or worked in adult ministries.

APs face a challenge of moving their churches' visions forward with uncooperative volunteers. Noah expressed this problem as a dance between pursuing alignment while not alienating long-serving volunteers, though they were difficult. His solution was to tell uncooperative volunteers, "You just keep doing what you are doing, and I'll just ignore you." Brad felt a frustration with uncooperative volunteers not creating relational space for new attenders by making friends: "When I show them a name and say, 'Let's reach out to this person or pray for this person,' it's like, 'Oh my gosh, well I don't know that person.'"

Key Leaders Have Mixed Perceptions of Associate Pastors

At the top of the organization, APs were almost always perceived as pastors. At the bottom of the organization, at the congregational level, this was not always the case. Associate pastors were often discounted their formal authority or pastoral recognition. This was a key problem for many associate pastors. For example Isaac, while chairing a committee meeting, was told by one of the participants, "I just want you to know, you are not my pastor." Noah, when asked, "What does it look like to be an associate pastor in your congregation?" responded, "I think it looks like a just small step above a volunteer leader." He felt APs did not get the same respect as the SP.

Youth pastors often did not feel that the congregation viewed them as a pastor, particularly when their roles changed or grew beyond youth. Though their former teenagers perceived the greater responsibility and authority of the new role, parents had a much more difficult time handling the transition. Noah particularly noted his former youth ministry students saw him as a pastor while their parents had not: "[The teenagers] seem to have made that transition with me a lot easier than some of the parents." APs might require their SPs to reemphasize their pastoral position with congregants. For instance, when Sam had a dispute with some of his youth group members, they went over his head to complain to his SP, but the SP sent them back to Sam to work out the problem.

Reciprocating Trust with Volunteers

APs said that relationships of trust with volunteers are crucial to ministry effectiveness. An AP's willingness to give ownership to volunteers without micromanaging is one example of that trust. Sam was learning how to give more ownership to volunteers: "And when do I need to take my hands off and say, 'We don't get enough ownership from the staff and is that my fault'?"

Trust could revolve around a particular skill set, such as competency to teach the Bible or ability to lead worship. For example, Alex learned he had to trust the gifts of his volunteers: "The moment I try to regulate that, I've now become the small opening that they have to try to fit through. Take the lid off. Let them go!" Eric's trust of volunteers was based on their ability to lead; he particularly measured their competence and confidence as a mark of how much trust they could be given in a ministry. However, more often trust revolved around relational dynamics. For example, Colin found that by developing rich friendships that included eating, playing, and spending time together, it was simpler to develop relationships of trust with his youth counselors: "It's pretty important that we actually like each other."

Frameworks of Associate Pastor Complexity

Figure 5-4 describes the relational complexity that many APs navigate in their pastoral duties within their congregations. APs navigate tensions between SPs and boards; between boards and their congregations; between their SP and key leaders, particularly when it comes to their authority and power as a pastor; and between key leaders and congregants. Usually, at the top of the organization, SPs and boards recognize APs as pastors, but leaders and congregants may not always see the AP in the same way.

What makes this relational web even more complex is that participants can occupy multiple places in the framework at once. For example, one of Alex's elders also served as one of his youth ministry volunteers. Alex called this phenomenon an "interwebbing," or webs of relationships.

While the framework of Figure 5-4 describes how most APs experienced complexity in their congregations, some APs described frameworks with different relational tensions. For example, while Figure 5-3 described APs with strong elder boards, Jenna suggested that her church board was much weaker and held little influence over her pastor. When asked to clarify, she described a structure where the associate pastor remained in the middle, but the SP was connected directly to the congregation and to the key leaders.

Two APs described the significant influence of an exterior bishop on their congregation and on their placement within the congregation. When asked what drew her to pastoral care and missions, Caroline answered that she wasn't and had been placed by her bishop, inheriting the role of the previous AP. Becca was nervous about being reappointed by her bishop to a church that needed new leadership, and feared the collapse of a new ministry she had been working to develop with unchurched young adults in her current context.

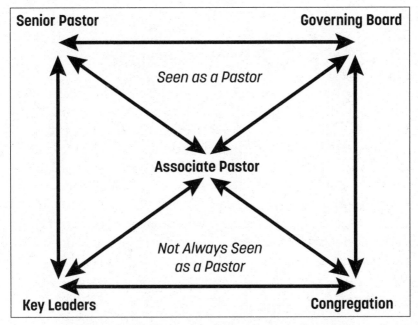

**Figure 5-4: Senior Pastor, Board, Congregation,
and Key Leader Relationships**

APs who were youth pastors described an additional set of relationships with parents. Alex, for example, felt it one of his responsibilities as the youth pastor to disciple parents to equip their own children. Sam, Alex, and Colin, and Henry all had to orient parents to the ministry's purposes and vision. Henry established a steering committee with parents and volunteers to set direction for the youth. Frank, on the other hand, had little positive or negative feedback from parents, forcing him to rely on volunteers to give adequate feedback to the ministry's performance. Figure 5-5 includes a diagram showing the relational complexity experienced by youth pastors.

Another framework described by associate pastors was congregations with significant executive pastors. Paul himself occupied this role. Owen relied on his executive pastor to give direction to the ministry when his SP could not cast vision. Greg and Isaac were in a similar situation, and relied on the feedback of their SP. Amy, while not the executive pastor, functioned as one for her fellow staff when her SP was absent from the office and could not provide clarity.

Table 5-1 displays the number of participants who described their participation in the different organizational structures. While in this particular study a governing board was described most clearly, the APs who participated in the study highly influenced the salience of the governing board framework. If the study had focused on episcopal (bishop-led) churches, it might be that the external bishop framework would have been more dominant. If APs from larger megachurches had been included, it may be that the executive pastor framework would have been more dominant. Nonetheless, what is common to all of these frameworks is that associate pastors are squarely in the middle of their congregational organizations.

Table 5-1: Participants Describing Associate Pastor Frameworks[2]

Governing Board	Weak or No Board	External Bishop	Youth Pastor	Executive Pastor
10	1	2	7	7

---

2   The numbers in this table corresponding to Figure 5-4 in the case of those who had governing boards and to Figure 5-5 in all other cases. The number of participant descriptions totals twenty-seven. While there were only twenty-five participants in the study, two participants described both executive pastor and youth pastor relationships within their role, and so are counted twice.

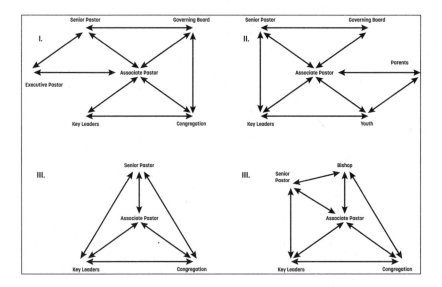

Figure 5-5: Other Associate Pastor Congregational Frameworks

Conclusion

Owen, in a focus group meeting, summarized well the challenge of the AP positions: "I think one of the toughest parts of our job is that we are pinched, however you draw it." APs navigate a web of complexity in their congregations that place them between the various constituencies of their churches. The middle position which APs occupy gives them opportunities to influence learning in the congregation while presenting personal learning challenges that APs must confront in order to facilitate others' learning.

CHAPTER 6

Learning Wide and Deep Roles

If you have ever been to Paris, you know that it is a city of huge boulevards that connect the beautiful landmarks spread across the landscape to one another. It is also a city of small winding alleys, tight turns, and dense neighborhoods. But if you get lost, all you have to do is look up, find a tall spire or dome, and walk toward it. Soon enough, you'll be out in the open and lined up on the boulevards.

In the last chapter, we looked at how associate pastors put a map on the dense and complex relationships in their congregations so that they don't get lost. They use this map as a way of making clear connections between significant responsibilities that they have toward key constituents in their congregations. These relationships put them at the direct center of the congregation. They can clearly see both the "top" of the congregation at the senior pastor and board level, and the "bottom" with key leaders and the general congregation. To continue with our topographic metaphor, associate pastors function as their church's "town square" where all the roads in the congregation converge. They are at the nexus of all the relationships in the church.

Just as you can find lots of different street vendors selling food, clothing, sunglasses, souvenirs, maps, and even tours in a town square, you find all sorts of responsibilities finding their way to the associate pastor's desk. Despite different job descriptions, they have vast responsibilities in their churches and need ways of thinking about what they do and who they are doing it for. One could describe their work as *wide* in terms of the different specific responsibilities, and *deep* in terms of the roles they play in relation to the responsibilities and the relationships they have above, beside, and below them in the congregation's structure.

This chapter now describes how associate pastors understand their job descriptions and then manage their learning in their congregations in light of those responsibilities by asking the question: "How do associate pastors facilitate their own learning in the congregational system?"

Deep and Wide Responsibilities and Roles

In just about every desk, there's a drawer where everything important and unimportant is hidden or stored: favorite pens, keys, erasers, rolls of quarters, business cards, highlighters, old buttons, three-by-five cards, and staples. It is an all-purpose toolbox where you stick anything and everything. It does the vast majority of the storage work of your desk.

The junk drawer is a consistent metaphor that associate pastors use to describe their job descriptions and roles in their congregations:

"My job is the junk drawer of the church."

"I'm the everything guy."

"I'm the Swiss Army knife of the church . . . most things are going to funnel into me."

"I do whatever my SP doesn't want to do."

For these APs, a giant span of relationships was often paired with a giant span of pastoral responsibilities and tasks. On the one hand, the APs' duties were organizationally deep since they involved various levels of the congregation, and on the other hand their duties were wide since their job descriptions covered many areas of ministry and church life.

Wide in Managing Ministries

For example, Henry, when asked what responsibilities he had for the church said, "Um, it's pretty much . . . everything!" John also described a large role but with a specific focus: "So, my role is to oversee, really, any education. But small groups, but that's probably the biggest chunk." Becca described her role in a similar way: "I was appointed to oversee all discipleship ministry from birth to death." While not personally directing all of the ministries, Becca did oversee all the ministry staff. Likewise, Kathy oversaw almost all of the discipleship staff in her church, managed programming, and ensured that details were communicated to the parish administrator.

While APs often enter congregations in a specific ministry, their job descriptions can grow as their responsibilities either evolve gradually or suddenly shift. For example, Brad described the evolution of his job description from youth and family to community life: "Basically, I'm just doing everything that I used to do but I'm now overseeing the life group and small group ministry, and the assimilation process." Even APs who had tightly defined roles, such as Farrah the music minister, still had responsibilities that lay outside of their specific ministry, like pastoral care.

Deep in Roles Throughout the Congregation

Married couples take on different roles with their family members. Husbands and wives are at once lovers, supporters, and sounding boards to their spouses while also teaching, coaching, disciplining, and advising their children, all while making decisions for their aging parents. These roles don't account for all their responsibilities but do give shape to how they perform them with every person in their family context.

The stories above explain the width of APs' responsibilities, but these responsibilities require that APs perform different roles as visionaries, managers, teachers, and one-on-one disciplers. Rather like married couples, these roles give shape to their relationships throughout their congregations and come with tensions and complexities of their own. Associate pastors see these roles as inherently relational. No element of their work is strictly a task; every job carries significant relational weight that they carry throughout the system of the congregation.

Associate Pastors as Visionaries

APs are often vision-casters in their ministries, providing direction for their volunteers. Noah found himself casting a vision for multiplying missional small groups in his congregation, though he

did this in the absence of his SP casting a vision. Carol developed a
vision for increasing the capacity of the church's pastoral care, again
because there had been an absence of vision. Becca developed a new
vision for small groups for non-Christian discipleship using spiritual
formation questions. However, she was nervous about being seen as
a vision-caster and how that might put her in tension with her SP.

Associate Pastors as Managers

Walk into an AP's office and a calendar will be hanging prom-
inently on the wall, marked with events in every imaginable color.
Such a calendar demonstrates that APs are managers of their congregations—and APs were not afraid to identify themselves as such. Becca,
for example, said, "My position seems to be a little more management
in the sense of management and oversight of staff." Eric said, "In
our congregation, my role is a lot of project management, a lot of
facilitating, because we do have strong leaders." Logan stated, "Administration is a big part of my role. If we're doing any events, that's
a big part of my role." John had also had diverse roles over volunteers
but also oversaw the library, website, and curriculum purchases. Colin
had to learn to appreciate the administrative management side of his
role as significant to his ministry, confessing that he much preferred
discipleship to management.

The Difference Between Visionary and Manager

APs perceived a split between vision-casting and managing, with
the former task belonging to the SP role and management being the
AP's role. Logan, for example, said, "[My SP] is kind of the visionary guy and I'm the detail guy." Owen felt that as the AP, he did not
have the necessary creative or imaginative capacities necessary to be
the primary vision-caster that was needed to be a SP, and that he was
more management-oriented. Kathy also saw the dichotomy occurring
around the idea of creativity: "He has lots of ideas; I'm more thinking
about the details and the administrative pieces."

Reese felt that he was not encouraged to be a visionary and described his AP role through three metaphors. First, he was baseball

outfielder who caught routine fly balls. Second, he was first officer of the ship to the SP's captain: "The elders will lead, the SP will steer the ship, and you will be a good first mate." Third, he used the metaphor of terrain as he remembered his SP's instruction to him: "I don't need you to go move into new terrain; I need you to make sure the terrain we're in continues to hold together." Both Reese and Becca talked about protecting the SP as a function of management. Becca, when describing former roles as an AP, particularly talked about protecting the SP's time for sermon prep, worship planning, and vision-casting.

On the other hand, Colin described the perceived dichotomy between vision-casting and managing as false. He saw vision-casting occurring at both levels of the organization versus being locked into a single position: "The lead pastor would have general goals for the entire church that he feels like the Lord is wanting us to go toward, and then he kind of leaves it for the associate pastors to figure out that takes—to shape and form it in their specific congregation."

When Senior Pastors Don't Cast Vision

While APs were loyal to their SPs and their vision, they experienced frustration when SPs struggled to cast vision or when there was conflict around the vision itself. Noah, for example, was frustrated that his SP didn't have a vision for the church and was unsure about pushing his own vision, "because our SP basically will say, 'Yeah! Whatever you want.'" Alex noted that his SP, after accomplishing a series of goals in the first part of his ministry, was disengaging in staff meetings and leaving the executive pastor to run staff meetings. "And so, [the SP] is not the vision guy either. And I think he is trying to get vision taken off of his job description." Greg felt that his church staff were not bound together because of the SP's lack of vision. Isaac likewise described his previous SP as a gifted preacher who was disconnected from the church's ministries, and left it to Isaac to discern his own ministry's vision. He hoped his new SP would give more direction. "He was always there to help if I needed it, but you're pretty much on your own. I think with this new [SP], we are hoping that he is pushing a little bit more of a vision."

Becca saw her lack of professional development in relationship to her fear of overstepping a professional boundary and competing for the spotlight with her SP. She explained this as an anxiety of getting into a power play with the SP about decision-making and leadership, which she had seen with other APs in her denomination. She viewed this as equally problematic for church congregants who would be drawn into the ambiguity of the power dynamic. Her current SP has been more supportive of her role than previous SPs, and she is working to change her perspective on professional development. "I'm learning that that's backwards in its own way; that I don't have to be fully submissive to just a sort of worker-bee position."

Associate Pastors as Teachers or One-on-One Disciplers

While management was a common theme in the interviews, APs also still had direct responsibilities for preaching, teaching, and discipling. These responsibilities could occur in the realm of small group leadership, adult or youth education classes including Sunday school, or in one-on-one relationships in the context of discipleship, spiritual formation, catechesis, or counseling. Paul, a youth pastor, called such a posture and position the player-coach:

> This is where you are building relationships, and you know eventually stuff will come out as kids are sharing, whether it is in response to a question or life issues that come up. As a youth pastor, you are kind of a player-coach, and in some ways you need to be more of a coach, and be there to support your leaders.

In such roles, APs work to establish a model for other key leaders, volunteers, or staff to follow.

APs find delight and energy in serving as teachers and disciplers. Alex loved having students come in and out of his office. Frank was working with young people who had started in his youth group and had become college students who needed basic catechesis. Becca was responsible for planning and executing the worship at her church, which required her involvement as a preacher. Sam and Mark both led weekly Sunday adult classes at their churches. John described two very intentional relationships with congregants: a thirtysomething young man who recently converted to Christianity, and a forty-year-old pastor who went through a painful departure from his church. Micah described very intense relationships that he had with the men he ministered at his church's outreach ministry, where he modeled mature Christian adulthood for former prison inmates.

Associate Pastors at the Boundary of the Congregation

APs also function in one additional area: they are networkers at the boundary of the congregation. Here, APs establish connections with other institutions or service organizations to develop networks or help people in need. Micah's ministry required him to network with the Illinois Department of Corrections. Diane and Erin both worked extensively with hospice centers and hospitals. Erin worked to establish a ministry in a local jail, taking care of female inmates. Amy also did jail ministry, preaching and teaching at a women's prison. Logan routinely worked with homeless people who came to the door needing help, and knew the location of shelters in the vicinity of his congregation.

Three Factors That Motivate
Associate Pastors to Learn

APs can be easily overwhelmed by the tide of their responsibilities as visionaries, managers, teachers, and community ambassadors. Becca used the metaphors of spinning plates and juggling balls to describe prioritizing responsibilities: "Right now, the best I can do is to keep the balls in the air that are of the utmost priority, meaning, even if this ball dropped, *this* ball cannot drop. Now, these other balls are important, but right now, they can go."

APs described the need to be self-motivated, to make sense of opportunities and responsibilities and to provide some definition to their own roles. Henry described himself as an entrepreneur in ministry, needing freedom to define his ministry and press into new areas of growth. Frank noted that in his ministry, since nobody was looking over his shoulder, it would be easy to get lazy, so self-motivation was critical to the role. Eric described self-motivation as necessary for creating a cohesive vision for in the AP ministry in the face of congregational criticism: "You have to be a self-starter, because nobody understands your job. The congregation doesn't understand. They think they know what you do all week. They don't know. So you have to have a lot of vision. You have to take charge."

Now that we have seen what associate pastors do, we can ask how they learn to do it by answering the question: "How do associate pastors facilitate their own learning in their congregations?" To quickly review, associate pastors have many responsibilities, and associate pastors don't separate tasks from the people they serve in the system. Every task has relational weight, which shapes how associate pastors accomplish what they do.

With that being the case, associate pastors describe three motivating factors for their ministries. First, since associate pastors have a lot to do, it is not surprising that when they seek to facilitate their own learning that they seek to sharpen their ministry skills as they manage the width of what they do. However, since they these tasks are relational, they also describe the following two motivations. Second, they learn to manage the relational anxiety these relationships create. Third, they also seek to verify their calling as pastors.

Sharpening Ministry Skills

APs discovered the need to sharpen their preaching, teaching, and other pastoral skills acquired in seminary, but they also discovered the need to develop new skills in management and leadership in order to fulfill their pastoral duties and job descriptions. For example, Colin described the need to sharpen ministry skills as he experienced "firecrackers going off" in the first couple of years in his ministry. He realized that his deficits in management did not help him facilitate discipleship and teaching. Alex and Sam commented that learning management skills and sharpening teaching skills might provide relief for anxiety in ministry. Sam stated, "You know, certainly, increasing competency helps calm anxiety."

APs were frustrated that these skills had to be learned on the job. Take, for example, this exchange between Owen and Jenna in a focus group over having to teach themselves how people learn and educational foundations once they had begun their pastorates in their congregations:

Owen: We, especially in seminary, we learn how to preach and handle the Word. Foundational, very important. But sometimes I feel like professors themselves, or even in the curriculum, forget that there is tons of literature on education and how people learn.

Jenna: Yeah.

Owen: And we don't touch that.

Jenna: There's a lot of tools.

Owen: Yeah, like, my senior pastor literally said to me, "Well the reason you don't learn that in seminary is because you can learn that out in the world, you can learn that at your church."

Jenna: (Laughs) Yes, in all my spare time!

Owen: Yeah, yeah. What?

Colin: You learn that by trial by fire (Laughs)!

Owen: Yes!!! And that is an approach to education.

Jenna: (Laughs) The thrown-in-the-deep-end approach.

Learning to Handle Anxiety

APs were not immune to the anxiety that can come from being pinched and from the pressures of stressful relationships and situations. There is an elegant symmetry that some APs pursued relationships with counselors as a way of handling personal anxiety. Jenna remembered being helped by counseling to overcome depression. Owen went to a counselor, since he struggled with fear: "What I am afraid of is being viewed as an idiot, or not being what I need to be, in order to get the job done." Paul pursued professional development to help him deal with burnout, taking a summer off to help recuperate.

Other APs managed their anxiety by engaging in spiritual disciplines. For example, Amy managed her workload through prayer: "Prayer is a big part of my life. I know I can't do any of this. I can't go into this without having prayed and asking God to give me direction." As Sam experienced intense anxiety when resistance came either from leadership above or from key leaders below, he would take time to withdraw and calm down by going home and sitting in a favorite chair to reflect and pray. Owen, who was stressed about appearing foolish and not up to the task as a pastor, would start every day with prayer: "Every day I try to start in confession. I can't do this on my own power. I don't actually have the skills to do it and any of the goals I have are nothing. It's all chaff, if it's not the Lord."

Greg noticed that working through anxiety enabled him to connect to other people's hurt. Greg shared, "I struggled with anxiety and depression. And God has used that to soften me so much, to feel the hurt of people." Jenna had a similar experience to Greg. "With counseling, I've learned a lot through counseling for ministry purposes. Emotional and spiritual health go together."

Verification of Calling

APs, surprisingly, did not talk extensively about ordination. However, verification of calling was a theme for female APs. Erin spoke about transitioning from being a lay volunteer to an ordained pastor in her denomination, as the completion of her educational tasks with children and youth at confirmation: "And so for me, that was a big piece; that sacramental piece of being able to not only teach about baptism but to celebrate baptisms and to celebrate the Lord's Supper was a very key piece."

Kathy discussed how it took her time and experience to feel like she had transitioned into a pastoral identity. She described how she would identify herself as a teacher, and that it took a long time for her to say she was a pastor. For her, it was a combination of time and experience: "more time preaching, more time interacting with the congregation members, doing the funerals, being at bedsides, praying."

Paul was thoughtfully considering whether it was time for him to evaluate a change in his calling. By utilizing reading, particularly the S.H.A.P.E.[1] materials from Saddleback Church, he attempted to think through whether or not he ought to remain in associate ministry or consider making a shift to a senior pastorate.

Finding Wisdom to Be an Associate Pastor: Practices That Strengthen Ministry Skills and Relationships

My neighbor is a landscaper who used to take care of my property. When I bought the house, he introduced himself, and told me all about the property and why the previous owner planted certain flowers or laid down the drainage pipe where he did. I realized he had significant knowledge that I lacked about my garden. He's busy, and we often only see each other either at the start or end of long days. But we shake hands, chat, and I get a chance to ask questions that keep my yard alive.

Above we saw three motivating factors that push associate pastors to learn. But associate pastors need more than motivation; they need sources of wisdom that strengthen skills and deepen relationships within their congregations. With that in mind, we can examine four primary practices that associate pastors pursue to facilitate their own learning: reading theology and leadership literature, pursuing theological education, developing an array of mentors, and attending conferences and ministerial groups. Note that these four means are not simply about learning to accomplish tasks; rather, they are about learning to work in relationships in their contexts by seeking wisdom in relationships.

---

1   Rees, S.*H.A.P.E.*

Reading Theology and Leadership Literature

APs seem to read incessantly. Their offices often contain a wall crammed with theology books and commentaries. One said succinctly, "I'm an avid reader." Another AP stated, "There's no end to the amount of books that I read. I'm a reader." Carol's personal goal was to read a book every month about leadership, ministry, or congregational care. Other APs are required by their SPs to set aside time for reading. John said, "But also, kind of in my personal goals with the church with my [SP], he's holding me accountable to, at minimum, one day a month of just study, reading. He'll encourage me to do it, weekly."

Some APs focus their attention on reading for spiritual growth. Greg intentionally studied what he termed "mystical" theological writers such as Tozer and Madame Guyon as a way of breathing life into what he considered "dry, dead" evangelicalism. Sam attempted to focus on reading what he referred to as "Scripture-soaked" theology books, for the sake of his spiritual growth and pastoral presence. Alex and Frank read theology to help their congregations think through sexual ethics.

Several APs read management and leadership ministry materials to make up a skill deficit upon entering their jobs. Eric studied secular management books because he felt he wasn't a very good manager. Colin emailed a former professor and asked for a bibliography of leadership and congregational culture books: "He just gave me a brief bibliography, I purchased all those books off Amazon, and went through all those." Paul read in order to help deal with anxiety about managing churches and burnout at midlife.

APs also make use of podcasts and other online applications to listen to sermons. Noah was very proud of his early adaptability to online sermons and podcasts; Alex, Frank, Brad were all prolific users of podcasts. Eric regularly listened to podcasts that dealt with management.

Pursuing Theological Education

APs pursue theological education to promote their professional development. Seminary was a vital experience for APs who began ministry later in life. Since he did not graduate college with a theological degree, Logan was required to pursue seminary after his church hired him. He initially resisted more school, but he grew to appreciate seminary, especially when it strengthened his theology and his preaching. Likewise, when Erin left a cherished career to join a church's staff, she wanted to be hired as a pastor; the SP agreed, but required she go to seminary. Farrah, a music conductor, also had a midlife call to ministry. She believed seminary confirmed her calling as she developed a clear philosophy of ministry and worship. When asked what her next step in professional development might be, Becca whispered, "Oh, my gosh! I think it would be the pursuit of education. Maybe actually in another degree. I can't believe I am saying that out loud." While Owen was adamantly against returning to seminary for a theology degree, he had given serious thought to pursuing an MBA.

Two APs didn't stop at a master's degree but went on for doctorates. Alex was motivated by his love of the classroom, though he didn't want an academic career. He enrolled in a modular DMin program to continue his pastoral development: "This isn't an academic degree; they are trying to make a reflective practitioner." Henry had mixed motivations for pursuing his doctorate. He wanted the degree to facilitate his own professional development in apologetics. Yet, since forty percent of his congregation had a doctorate, Henry felt that without the same degree he would not be recognized as an expert. Even the church's youth group believed Henry lacked credibility without the doctorate: "Even if it was a doctorate in, I don't know, car mechanics, if I just said 'I'm a doctor,' they would be like, 'Oh, wow, okay. I'll listen to what you have to say.'"

Developing an Array of Mentors

We've already seen that seeking relationships with counselors helps to manage anxieties. But APs also seek mentors to help them learn how to sharpen their ministry skills. Again, we're confronted with the reality that APs realize the relational heft of their responsibilities, and so they seek relationships with guides who can help them understand what they do and who they are. For APs, learning is rarely about just learning how to do a task—rather, it is about learning in relationship. Associate pastors look for such relationships with those embedded in the congregation, particularly in two places. First, they look for relationships with senior pastors. Second, they look for relationships with other associates and elders. But associate pastors also look for relationships with mentors outside the congregation. Thus APs seek triangulation[2] in their performance, by finding mentors who are both internal and external to their congregations.

Senior Pastors as Mentors

Some APs desired a mentoring relationship with their SP and found willing teachers. For example, Colin became close friends with his SP, who often invited him to his home for dinner and family game nights. John grieved deeply when his first SP died; he keenly felt the loss of a good mentor. Paul had a very long tenure with a single church and a single SP and found that the relationship had a sustaining effect on his ministry. Micah particularly viewed his relationship with his SP as more of a brotherhood than professional relationship: "I don't know that I could use the word 'work' to describe it."

Other Mentors from Inside the Congregation

Older APs on church staffs also serve as mentors for younger ones. Owen, struggling in his role, relied his executive pastor's coaching. Colin was very indebted to an older AP who served as a mentor in counseling teenagers: "[The older AP] has a counseling degree from his seminary, so I was in and out of his office like once a week . . . so just having him a resource has been super-helpful." Sam was specifically indebted to a particular elder who was a retired pastor who came alongside him: "I just went to him and said, 'You know, I just need somebody who's not on staff, that would be my pastor.'"

Mentors from Outside the Congregation

On occasion, associate pastors look for mentors outside of their church to help them with their growth. APs may hire professional

---

2   Triangulation is a navigational term that refers to the process by which a sailor, taking measurements from multiple landmarks, is able to calculate the position of his or her ship. Here, it is used to describe how an AP becomes sure of his or her responsibilities.

coaches to give them a hand. Colin reached back and asked for assistance from a previous seminary professor when a former SP was unwilling and unavailable to coach him in organizational management. Frank's congregation paid for him to hire a leadership coach with pastoral experience in California: "He's been there, walked through it, and I need someone to kind of shoot me straight. If I'm thinking something wrong or if I'm just way off base about something, he's someone who can come along and just be like, 'No, do it this way.'"

John spoke regularly with his father, who is a business coach: "About every two to three weeks we'll talk, and he helps me with time management, which is huge for me." Jenna wished for external coaches who could push her to learn other ways of thinking: "I'm mindful that there could be some other voices that I could learn from as well. Maybe it's time to ask for the money for that or make the space for that."

Attending Conferences and Ministerials

APs attended conferences and ministerials to facilitate their learning and to find supportive relationships with other APs. While most APs think attending conferences are important, they are very selective about which conferences they attend, and the reasons change over the course of their pastorates. For example, new youth pastors attend youth ministry conferences, but they do not necessarily attend for the content, and often start attending other types of conferences. Sam particularly disliked youth conferences, since he felt that they exacerbated tensions with SPs and overexalted youth ministry. Alex used to attend a popular youth conference but switched to an academic theology conference: "I could keep my finger on the pulse of various things that were happening in the theological world, and that actually proved to be tremendous for my ministry here." Colin also attended academic conferences, but he was motivated not by the content of the conference as much as by the personal relationships and connections.

On the other hand, Paul regretted abandoning conferences, particularly after he was promoted away from youth ministry, and wished he had been more proactive in finding a conference that fit his niche as an executive pastor. Kathy experienced personal growth from such a niche conference that specifically focused on women in ministry. Eric routinely attended management seminars in an effort to improve his management abilities. Noah attended conferences that focused on disciplemaking. Carol was admitted to a fellowship that sponsored three conferences on leadership around the country for young ordained clergy.

Local ministerial groups were also important for many APs. Logan loved meeting with other pastors in his denomination's ministerials. Another denomination provided learning cohorts that Noah and Owen appreciated, in order to learn about missional communities. However, ministerials were particularly important for APs who were minorities or female. Kathy spoke about a ministerial that was intentionally for new young clergy members that met twice a year. Jenna described being in an online group for women pastors where she could ask questions of other female pastors. Colin, not finding a ministerial that met the specific needs of Chinese APs, collaborated with others to develop a very specific ministerial for Chinese youth pastors.

Conclusion

AP's ministries are spread over a broad area of responsibilities and have depth in relation to vision-casting, managing, teaching and discipling, and working at the boundaries of their congregations. APs work hard to sharpen skills, calm anxieties, and verify calling through a wide range of strategies including reading, higher education, and gathering with other APs at conferences and ministerial groups. Through facilitating their own learning, APs gain the skills necessary to facilitate the learning of the other members of the congregational systems they serve. The next chapter examines how APs facilitate such learning with their fellow congregational members.

CHAPTER 7

Associate Pastors as Player-Coaches

My brother-in-law Justin is a farmer, and his implement shed is full of all kinds of tractors. I had no idea they could come in so many varieties. Like many farmers, Justin keeps some tractors for sentimental reasons. The old antique that Grandpa Russell used is parked next to several newer models. But Justin has one tractor that is the workhorse of his fleet. It runs most of the time and can pull the auger, planter, sprayer, tiller, and water tank. This tractor is the go-to, the "old reliable." When it eventually breaks down permanently, it will bring a tear to Justin's eye. It simply can't be done without.

In the last chapter, we saw that associate pastors are the workhorses of their congregations. Their churches can't get by without them. They are responsible for the vast majority of day-to-day responsibilities of a church; and as the last chapter described, this can include anything from ordering stir rods to casting vision for new ministries and de-termining which programs remain operative. In addition, they have to constantly facilitate their own learning to make their ministries work while staying spiritually healthy.

Just as no farmer can get by with one tractor, no church can op-erate with just one workhorse. Associate pastors realize that they are responsible for teaching, training, and equipping the congregation to grow in Christlikeness and fulfill the vision and mission of the congregation. How associate pastors go about this responsibility is likely unique to their congregation's culture and setting.

To borrow from what youth pastor Paul said in the previous chapter, associate pastors are player-coaches. They are the quarterback on a football team who can see the field, the opposing team, and the end zone. While everyone else is focused on a specific task, the associate pastor calls plays that facilitate gaining yards and scoring points. These plays orchestrate how the different players move in relationship to the quarterback and the goal. Yet at the same time, the associate pastor is like the coach on the sidelines, who has been training the team to kick field goals, block tacklers, clear lanes, and run with the ball to score.

The associate pastor is the player-coach who facilitates the whole congregation's learning in the middle of a complex and ambiguous environment. It is here most of all where the associate pastor needs the flexibility and freedom to accomplish the vision of the church. As Paul said of his church, there is a need for "room to run."

This chapter answers the question, "How do associate pastors facilitate the congregation's learning?" Initially, associate pastors often confront a culture of unintentional learning which must be overcome. Then, they rely on a diverse set of strategies to respond to their congregation's learning needs.

When I reviewed the diverse answers to this part of the study in a focus group with associate pastors, I noted that initially the responses felt a touch haphazard. Alex, knowing that congregations are often ambiguous, replied, "It makes sense that this section is a little more scattershot." One size doesn't fit all when it comes to facilitating learning in congregations. Nonetheless, the strategies utilized by APs followed a pattern of using orientation points to facilitate learning, managing tensions while facilitating learning, and implementing practices in facilitating learning.

Some Congregations Struggle with Intentional Learning

Parker Palmer describes education as "creating spaces where obedience to the truth can be practiced."[1] Such a definition of education

---

1   Palmer, *To Know as We Are Known.* 69.

suggests that without the intentional making of such space, relationships that practice the truth are impossible. Such spaces have a clear commitment to truth in relationship and the practice of that truth in the shared, lived world. Such learning is intentionally guided by the community and its teachers.

Congregations are certainly "spaces where obedience to the truth can be practiced." Yet associate pastors were often unsure of how intentional their congregations were at setting learning goals. Look at how they answered the question: "How does your congregation set intentional learning goals?"

"They don't. I don't think we do. I don't think we have learning goals."

"It's somewhat intentional."

"They don't. We don't."

"Hmm . . . wow . . . I don't think I've ever thought of youth ministry as setting specific goals."

"That is definitely a 'want' in our congregation at best."

"I would say average at best, honestly."

"I don't think we're very intentional, in setting goals."

These replies did not mean learning was not taking place. Indeed, as we've seen, APs recount long lists of programs, classes, and learning activities. Their frustration was not in a lack of learning—rather, that setting explicit learning goals for the congregation was not often a high priority for congregational boards and leaders at the top of the organization, and that sometimes the setting of those goals was rather haphazard. When this happened, APs often filled in the gaps to set intentional goals for learning.

For example, Brad planned to respond to the intentionality gap in his congregation by working to develop a disciplemaking culture. Similarly, Noah's primary goal for learning was developing missional communities that introduced neighbors to the gospel:

We don't see a lot of people reaching out to nonbelieving friends or family. They don't have a deep conviction to do that. So I began exploring different things to try to answer that problem, and a lot of things really clicked with me with the whole missional community way of living.

Associate Pastors Use a Variety of Orientation Points to Facilitate Learning

If you've ever gone golfing, you know that the goal of the game is to get the ball in the hole in as few shots as possible. But sometimes the green is far away or obscured by a hill, and golfers can't see the hole. When that happens, golfers rely on some key orientation points. The first is the flag which rests in the hole. If the golfers can see the flag, they at least know the direction of the hole. The second is the score card, which has a map that golfers can use to get a sense of the terrain. The third are the distance markers, which are colored concrete pads or posts which indicate the remaining distance to the hole. While the golfer can't always see the hole, these three orientation points give him or her an awareness of where to hit the ball, with what club, and with what amount of force.

APs were able to guide their learning practices toward either explicit or implicit goals through specific learning practices and strategies. In order to facilitate learning, APs required some orienting marks for their congregations in order to facilitate learning. Three common orienting points were biblical texts, the vision of the church, and a profile of a mature disciple.

Orienting to Biblical Texts

Congregations had broad learning goals that often fell under three general scriptural and theological categories. First, congregations often oriented learning goals to the greatest and second greatest commandments of the Old Testament law (Lev. 19:18; Deut. 6:1–4) and toward Jesus's teaching of the same (Mark 12:29–31). Second, congregations were oriented to the Great Commission or to evangelistic effort (Matt. 28:18–20). Third, congregations were oriented to equipping the saints for acts of service in the broader church environment (Eph. 4:11–16). Further, APs described their churches as biblically oriented and evangelical, preaching and teaching the Bible. Teaching the entire canon of Scripture was an explicit goal.

Orienting to the Church's Vision

Some churches intentionally align learning and ministry with their church's vision for ministry. Becca stated succinctly, "In my experience, most churches have no idea what their mission is. They've not named it clearly and they don't take ownership in it." But where vision and mission were clear, APs had a better chance of orienting ministry well. For example, John's church worked toward a family-oriented ministry with the three emphases of Sunday worship, small group ministry, and family worship. Sam's church had a crisp vision statement: "A reading, preaching, teaching church: Christian minds in the making." Consequently, Sam often assigned reading to students and those seeking pastoral care. Carol's ministry was organized to help move her church to a more missional status using a step-by-step immersive approach that began with creating sandwiches after Sunday worship, moved on to weekly events, and then ended with opportunities to take mission trips around the world.

Orienting to a Profile of a Mature Disciple

Alex's church spent considerable energy orienting learning toward the church's specific vision of a mature disciple. They developed a profile of a mature disciple that would guide the ministry of the church, moving with congregants from children's ministry through adulthood. All educational class offerings were aimed at producing fruit through a vision of maturity. Alex described the benefit of a well-designed curriculum as meaningful accomplishment of a model of discipleship: "Once you have the goal in mind, your curriculum is now aimed at that. So, we don't have classes for free. If you are meaningful about the classes that you take, within a fairly short amount of time you'll have direct teaching on all the things we think you need to hear, to become this mature believer in Christ."

Associate Pastors Facilitate Learning
by Managing Tensions

Ah, Saturdays! Finally, a day off. You can spend the day any way that you choose—until you remember that your neighbors would like you to spruce up your yard, you promised your children you would take them to the movies, you told your spouse you would pick up the groceries, and you need to have a long conversation with your parents. You only have twenty-four hours; which person or group will you satisfy in order to get some of these chores and responsibilities done? How will you navigate the tension of the limits of time and energy?

Associate pastors and congregations have limited time and resources, and associate pastors have to manage those resources by navigating tensions within the work congregation itself. There were four primary tensions that associate pastors encountered: ministry within the congregation versus ministry outside the congregation, centralized versus decentralized ministry, Sunday school versus small group ministry, and content versus practice.

Ministry Within versus Ministry Outside the Congregation

APs faced the tension of caring for congregational members within the ministries of the church while wanting to reach out to the surrounding communities in evangelism or outreach. APs named this tension in a variety of ways. Jenna described such a tension as a healing orientation versus an outward orientation. Jenna's church was a "contemplative community," where emotional health and spiritual healing were a part of the congregation's core identity and focused the church inwardly. Jenna's church is renovating a church in a suburban area, and this may cause the church to redefine its identity: "We will be at the center of a community. People will see the steeple and will know that this is a church."

John also struggled to help a portion of his congregation understand this tension. A homeschool consortium makes up a significant portion of his church's population. This population tries to orient their ministry toward the church's and town's homeschool community, while John and his SP wanted the church to provide a broader outreach to their industrial small town. An interchange between Sam and a congregant captured the tension: "I want us to have a good reputation. But I am more concerned how we are perceived in the community by the community—the actual community."

Carol was also pushing against a similar tension as she moved her ministries to be "less institutional, more missional." Carol noticed a pull in congregants toward an institutional mentality, where the church existed to meet the needs of members, rather than a missional mentality, where congregants would see the church as serving those who didn't know the Lord. In pushing for an orientation from inward to outward, Frank referred to growth groups as a "holy huddles." When asked what he would hope to see, he replied, "that community would almost be like a miniature church for them. So we would want that, but at the same time we want to be showing that life to nonbelievers." Noah described a similar tension that he faced with his small groups, which he explained as attractional versus missional. He felt the small group ministry had been very inward, and he was attempting to orient the ministry to be more outward by teaching and implanting strategies from his missional community readings: "If we can just turn them outward, even just a little bit, I think we'll start seeing conversion growth. We'll start seeing people interacting as a group, as a community, with nonbelievers."

Centralized versus Decentralized Ministry

Paul recognized another significant tension in his church: a ministry orientation that was centralized versus decentralized. A centralized ministry occurred at the church where pastoral staff had a lot of on-site control over the operation, whereas decentralized ministry was formal ministry happening off-site where it was harder to maintain control. Such ministries took place at volunteers' homes or in restaurants: "When you are trying to keep your finger on the pulse of what's happening, that's a little bit more challenging because it's a little harder to be eyes-on with that." Such ministries required an intense amount of trust.

Erin lamented that her care ministries were not more centralized and interwoven into the fabric of her church's ministries. Isaac's church moved their congregants through a discipleship pathway that went from a more centralized ministry to decentralized ministries. John, on the other hand, faced a different tension that could be described as structured versus organic. John's church had little centralized adult ministry and no children's ministry or youth ministry in the church. John described this as a family model with a heavy emphasis on small groups. When pushed on why no Sunday school, he stated, "I would like us to get there."

Sunday Morning Education versus Small Groups

Perhaps one of the most visible ways that APs facilitated learning was in the formal adult education offerings of a congregation with they either taught directly or oversaw. While some churches offered both adult level classes on Sunday mornings in the form of Adult Bible Fellowships (ABFs) or other types of gatherings and small group ministries, APs seemed to value one over the other.

Many APs valued Sunday morning education and remembered days when it was a more valued ministry format. Brad was frustrated by the lack of attendance of Sunday school: "I do think it is a valuable thing. I know, we are fighting that nobody wants to come. Time is now the ultimate essence, and people are very lucky to even get an hour." Brad saw it as an erosion of the church culture, where family members who no longer saw it as valuable made it less likely that other congregants in their church would participate in Sunday school either: "I was at churches where it was part of the culture, and as soon as it starts to get away from that it's hard to come back to it." Eric was passionate about adult education: "Sunday school is the most important ministry in the church, outside of the preaching. Worship service is the most important; Second to me is Sunday school. I really am a believer in Sunday school."

Greg's church had a successful Sunday morning ministry structure that went through intentional curriculum. Greg's concern was that the church had surrendered Christian education to the academy, and was not taking adequate responsibility for equipping Christians for ministry in their fields: "99.9% of your people have other careers. They've never really had teaching, education, training at [seminary] levels. So God never took away from the local church to do that."

On the other hand, other churches had tipped the scales toward almost exclusively small group offerings for their churches. Noah's church, for example, eliminated Sunday morning education to push people toward small groups. While not his decision, he supported the previous adult ministry pastor's decision to move away from a class-oriented ministry. Noah saw the biggest limitation to Sunday morning education as the number of people who could use their gifts in a given morning, allowing many people to spectate; whereas with small groups, larger numbers of people could employ their spiritual gifts regularly. Similarly, Logan focused on moving people into small groups for their primary discipleship. Becca's church also focused on small group classes: "So we've pulled the focus back in toward 'grow groups,' saying 'That is your first step, and maybe the only step you need in learning and discipleship.'"

Unlike most of the APs, Alex noted that his church had very distinct purposes for each ministry. Sunday classes were about equipping and learning, while small group ministries were about fellowship, connection, and prayer. Colin, having received new responsibilities in adult ministries, shared that his church discovered that small groups and classes were largely the same: "We actually had this discussion in our leadership meeting this past Wednesday night. But you know what? The difference between them is that one occurs on a Sunday and one occurs on a weeknight." Sam noted that he was in a tension between his SP and his board about which would be the preferred educational strategy. "Well, in [the SP's] case he's got a much more detailed plan, and it's very well thought-out. But almost to the person, the APs at the table, we think we need small groups."

Content versus Practice

APs were quite weary of having a content orientation to learning. They shared a perception that their congregations were far more concerned about doing Bible studies and ingesting Bible content than being obedient to or practicing Scripture. When asked about learning goals for the church, Brad said bluntly, "I guess, with that whole idea of learning, when I hear you say that word 'learning,' a lot of red flags go up for me." When asked to explain, Brad elaborated that for his congregation, learning revolved around biblical content rather than learning to be Christlike. Becca lamented the same insatiable appetite for Bible studies in her congregation: "And I say that not in a good way, because what it wasn't doing was leading to the tangible change in life transformation—that you also lived the things you were learning." Owen was equally frustrated with content-oriented consumption of Bible studies, wishing for an emphasis on reflection, while Paul hoped for an emphasis on application: "I'm passionate about seeing people apply whatever it is that they've learned, whether it is in a small group, or it is in the worship service, or wherever they are getting their material from."

On the other hand, some APs served congregations where the Bible was underutilized. Carol, for example, wanted to ensure that congregants who only participated on Sunday were able to hear the content of Scripture in worship and see themselves as a continuation of the story of Scripture. Carol was hopeful that preaching consistently from Scripture would provide more spiritual nourishment than her previous SP's self-help–oriented preaching. Kathy, likewise, wanted her church to be more biblically engaged.

Meanwhile, content continued to form an important element of catechesis and curriculum in AP ministry. John developed a recurring set of rotating classes that were designed to give a substantial overview to theology, including systematic theology and church history. Logan had a similar strategy in his church; classes in his rotation included prayer, mission, growth group ministry training, spiritual disciplines, conflict resolution, financial freedom, a study of Jesus's leadership methods, Bible studies, emotional health, evangelism training, and a study of *Experiencing God.* Greg's church had a robust curriculum based on hermeneutics—basically apologetics, doctrine, and evangelism. Amy also had a vision for leadership training based on intentional content that was skill-based. She hoped to teach prayer, Bible reading, and conflict resolution.

Sam and Alex had very intentional approaches to helping students go through the canon of Scripture in their youth ministry classes. Sam was particularly intentional about having students go through specific books such as John, Romans, Psalms, and Proverbs. Alex, likewise, moved through the canon of Scripture while teaching Christian worldview: "I'll alternate between the Old Testament and the New Testament because I want to get them in both testaments."

Associate Pastors' Practices to Facilitate Learning

When I ran cross-country in high school, our coach had a set of important drills that we would practice over and over. Mondays was always intervals day; we would practice running quarter- or half-mile repeats with minimal rest in between. Tuesday was mid-distance day; we would do a four-mile run at a brisk pace to mirror a race. Wednesday was hill day; we would run two miles to a hill, run up and down it ten times, and then run back to school. Thursday was a seven-mile run, and Friday was a slow three-mile jog. These recurring workouts, these practices, had the team ready for race day on Saturday.

So far in this chapter, we've seen that while not all congregations have specific learning goals, associate pastors creatively utilize orientation points and manage various congregational tensions to facilitate the learning of the congregational members. As we continue to utilize Paul's player-coach analogy, we could say that utilizing orientation points gives associate pastors a sense of the playing field, and that managing congregational tensions gives them a sense of the conditions on the field and what factors to weigh as they call the plays.

In the final section of this chapter, we'll examine specific practices that associate pastors employ to facilitate the learning of the entire congregation. We might consider these the actual plays the associate pastor calls as both coach and quarterback, as player-coach. In particular, we'll look at four key practices: APs facilitate learning by narrowing the focus, gathering groups to set direction, coaching key leaders, and acting as spiritual mentors.

Table 7-1: Associate Pastor Strategies for Facilitating Learning

Utilize Orientation Points	Manage Tensions	Practices
Biblical Texts	Ministry Within versus Outside the Congregation	Narrow the Focus
Congregational Vision	Centralized versus Decentralized Ministry	Gathering Groups to Set Direction
Picture of a Mature Disciple	Sunday school versus Small Groups	Coaching Key Leaders
	Content versus Practice	Acting as a Spiritual Mentor

Narrowing the Focus

Narrowing the focus by eliminating programming proved to be a significant way that APs worked to facilitate learning and focus the congregation. Jenna linked programming to the mission of the church: "It can be easy to do things just because you've done them, and not think about why, and what is the goal. Is it getting you somewhere?" Becca was not at all afraid to narrow the focus or to say no to ministries or events that lay outside of the ministry of the church; she described this emphasis on mission as a way of being clear on what ministries to say no to: "I cannot satisfy the needs of all people and stay on mission." She gave the example of denying funding or worship time for a children's drama team. While it was not a bad idea, she felt it did not help the church stay on mission to reach the community with the gospel. Narrowing the focus was a means of survival for Becca: "Even though our focus is narrowed,

I still have a hundred plates to spin." Becca used a narrowing focus strategy to avoid personal burnout and provide margin for a longer ministry career.

Isaac told the story of struggling to eliminate a camp ministry for his church, over the protest of his elders. Camp was expensive, and the congregation was attached to the camp because of their personal experiences of conversion or meeting spouses. After a dangerous fire, Isaac finally convinced his elder board to close the camp and start a different day camp ministry closer to the church. Colin shared about a traditional Chinese New Year program at his church that no longer resonated with the English-speaking portion of his church. Rather than continue in that program, he launched a Super Bowl party.

Gathering Groups to Set Direction

Some APs facilitated learning by gathering a whole team of volunteers together to discern the vision or direction for their ministry. Colin intentionally developed deep friendships with all of his youth volunteers by spending time training and equipping, as well as eating dinner and having fun with one another. As a result, he was able to develop the trust necessary to discern the direction of the ministry together. At the end of the school year, they would participate in an in-depth assessment of the ministry, in which they identified growth areas, potential leaders, and students who might need special assistance. Colin would then translate the meeting into a specific spiritual goal and align his teaching to the goal.

Irene was also able to draw on a team at the mid-level to facilitate learning. This form of facilitating learning depended on sharing a common vision and working together to come up with curriculum and classes for the church: "We've certainly had differences of opinion, and our pastoral staff has really worked hard on facilitating communication and having open conversation." Alex recounted how the previous AP convened a group of doctoral graduates in education and theology to set a picture of an idealized disciple, and the curriculum the church felt it would need to produce that disciple. Sam was trying to grow into a group-collaboration method as a pastor, but discovered they were slow to respond to questions about how they would like to be equipped for ministry: "And I've asked that question in the past, and normally just kind of get blank expressions." However, he had seen growth in the group selecting curriculum together.

Coaching Key Leaders

Not surprisingly, associate pastors spend a large amount of time coaching volunteers or subordinate staff members. While associates attempted to coach in groups, associate pastors seemed to prefer coaching one-on-one encounters with their volunteers or staff. Sometimes coaching is necessitated by the size and structure of a church. Carol's church, for example, had a coaching structure where she mentored five staff members on a monthly basis. Coaching included casting vision, talking through ideas, and troubleshooting problems.

Likewise, Becca spent most of her ministry time with mid-level staff, and described coaching as a process of direction and discernment. Discernment involved discovering how to equip teams, direct ministry, work with volunteers, and make necessary changes. Becca described her particular methodology in many cases of coaching as "defining the win." She shared how her small group team was tasked with developing a simple, attractive, and accessible onboarding strategy for new small group members.

Other APs like Noah spent considerable time coaching volunteers, particularly life group leaders, whom he met with as a group and coached individually in between meetings. Coaching for Noah consisted of training, course correcting, and praying: "Pray with them for their own ministry and life group leadership and what's going on in their lives as well." Kathy used the word "empower" to describe her interactions with key volunteers. She described interacting with a volunteer who was talented and excellent at his duties but often felt unsure about his performance: "We email back and forth a lot, and I support him, and encourage him in his leading, because he *is* an awesome leader."

John also primarily met with life group leaders. He characteristically described coaching as the full cycle of selection, training, and multiplication. John described a coaching relationship with a respect-ed leader for a new women's ministry. He first met with her weekly, then monthly, to hear out her ideas and jointly design the ministry: "Within that, the first thing I did in that was to ask her, 'How things are going: let's get the current state.' Then later, 'How things are going? What problems have you dealt with? What things have gone well?'" He would attempt to help her envision some potential positive and negative futures, while advising her to avoid reinventing the wheel.

Eric's style of coaching also exemplified this paradigm. He was very amiable to having volunteers come to him and pitch a vision for a specific ministry. He would then take a boilerplate template and orient the volunteer's ideas to the vision and mission of the church, and provide structure and accountability for the ministry.

Farrah coached her volunteers, giving strong parameters and guidance at first but then working to give them freedom to do things their way: "I want to give them as much freedom as I can." Alex had a very similar approach to coaching. After giving them the categories for how ministry works in the church and ministry, he attempted to step out of the volunteer's way.

Other associates, however, struggled with trust based on past experiences with volunteers or leaders hurting the congregation. John struggled to trust interns because of how his congregation had been treated by an outside interim pastor. John's trust increased as interns identified with the values and vision of the ministry, particularly in the areas of hermeneutics and counseling. Similarly, Sam's relational stance in coaching was one of relative distrust over potentially un-shared values. Amy noted that some APs she knew were afraid to coach volunteers for fear of the volunteers replacing them in their ministries.

Acting as Spiritual Mentors

While APs utilize coaching as a way of training volunteers, they also act as spiritual mentors in various relationships with their volun-teers. Greg noted that APs are exposed to the brokenness and pain of their congregants, and that pain needs to be addressed by God's grace and the Holy Spirit. Farrah, calling herself a spiritual counselor, said succinctly, "I get to be the God-interpreter." She described spiritual counseling as asking the question, "Where is God now? Where is God right now for you?" She also described counseling as helping people learn to act like adults.

Jenna preferred the term "spiritual direction." She described her gifts for listening, and high aptitudes for counseling, teaching, and creative expression, as essential in spiritual direction. Like Farrah, she pointed her congregants to the presence of God. "Sometimes it's a little bit of listening and helping them to point them to where God is, to where God might desire to take them, to speak words of encouragement and truth and love."

Reese described his vision of ministry almost entirely in language of spiritual formation. Reese desired to see his congregation express "an ease and a delight with God" that would be cultivated by spiritual disciplines such of prayer, Scripture reading, and creative engagement with God. Reese described this spiritual formation as distinct from Sunday worship and education, as it required vulnerable and authentic interactions in small groups or through one-on-one conversations.

Conclusion

The last three chapters have summarized the responses of twenty-five associate pastors to three pivotal questions: "How do you understand the complexity of your organization?" "How do you facilitate your own learning?" and "How do you facilitate the learning of others?" Owen summarizes the answers of the first question succinctly:

> Being an AP is not an easy position to be in, because you are kind of middle management. You work with volunteers, you work with the congregation, but then I have to report to an executive pastor and the elders. Sometimes you feel like you are in the middle, and it can get rough.

The pinched middleness can be very complex and ambiguous for associate pastors. Their relationship to all the various constituencies of their congregation place them squarely in the middle of the organizational dynamics while operating in a variety of capacities as visionaries, managers, teachers, and boundary workers, often at the same time. As a result, associate pastors must be self-motivated to bring their own definition to their roles, while facilitating their own learning to sharpen tools, confirm their own callings, and calm anxieties. Finally, associate pastors must utilize a variety of strategies to facilitate the learning of others in their congregations in an attempt to align them to the church's vision and mission.

If this is how associate pastors understand their position, are there any summary implications for how they operate in their congregations? The final chapter will suggest six key takeaways for associate pastors that will help them navigate the middle of their congregations as facilitators of learning.

CHAPTER 8

Six Critical Skills for Ministry in the Middle

M inistry is a maze made of people. Rather than negotiating walls and dead ends, associate pastors work with the complexity that is inherent when a diverse group of people gather together. Ministerial complexity houses ambiguous challenges that associate pastors must work through, to clarify the confusion that comes in congregational systems.

Being in the middle is fraught with the peril of pinchedness. However, middleness also comes with the possibility of power—a positive power that allows associate pastors to steward ambiguity through the role of the facilitator of learning. Associate pastors must accept the challenges of their middleness as possibilities for serving the congregation, by providing necessary clarity and by empowering members to pursue their God-given possibilities for ministry.

The associate pastors who participated in this study minister in congregations with diverse constituencies. Their stories and experiences point a way toward facilitating learning. They navigate the complexity and tensions between the different constituencies in their congregations, both at the top and bottom of the church as well as between members at the top and bottom of the church, and attempt to implement and clearly articulate the congregation's vision, develop trust with those above and below them, and take refuge with other associate staff in the middle of the organization.

Oshry describes organizational middleness as being in a hectic space, potentially ego-deflating, and confusing. Anyone in the middle of an organization, regardless of the kind of organization, experiences pressure from the top and the bottom which they perceive minimizes their power. So the middle can be a dis-integrating place, where organizational agents experience diffusion through the system.[1] However, Oshry writes:

> Diffusion is the source of the unique power of the middle. Diffusion provides contact with and information about different parts of the system, and it is that contact and information which makes it possible for Middles to see the total system more clearly than either Tops or Bottoms and which enables them to function in a sensitive and informed matter.[2]

As such, Oshry recommends that those in the middle see themselves as integrators of their systems,[3] and suggests that integration happens when there is a team of managers[4] who diffuse outward in the organization and then return to the middle to integrate the organization. When integration happens, the system experiences the positive consequences of greater consistency throughout the system, as all participants have information and resources necessary in order to perform their roles.[5] However, integrating is challenging because the middle position experiences pulls between "conflicting agendas, perspectives, priorities, needs, and the demands of two or more individuals or groups."[6]

Remember that in chapter 5 associate pastors described their significant relationships as a web of triangles in which the associate pastor was placed in the middle of the congregation. While these triangles depended on the framework of the church's polity and de-

---

1   Oshry, *In the Middle*, 9–10.
2   Oshry, *In the Middle*, 12.
3   Oshry, *In the Middle*, 44.
4   Oshry, *In the Middle*, 49.
5   Oshry, *In the Middle*, 53.
6   Oshry, *In the Middle*, 80.

nominational structure, usually associate pastors were positioned in four triangles: one including the senior pastor and the governing board members, one between the elder board and the congregation, one between the congregation and the key leaders or volunteers associate pastors relied upon, and finally between the key leadership and the senior pastor, as described below in Figure 8-1, though there were other configurations, as diagrammed in Figure 8-2.[7] Yet, regardless of the framework, associate pastors are "pinched" in every direction.

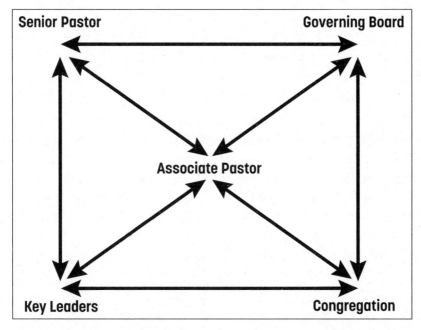

Figure 8-1: Associate Pastors with Governing Boards

---

7   Other frameworks either eliminated the relationship between the senior pastor and governing board; substituted a more lopsided triangle between the associate pastor, senior pastor, and exterior bishop; added an executive pastor position, or highlighted tensions between parents and youth (cf. Figure 8-2). As noted in chapter 5, the participating APs came primarily from congregational or Presbyterian polities with governing boards, and account for the prevalence of the governing board framework. Yet in all of the frameworks, the associate pastor is placed not only in the middle position of all the triangles, but in the middle of the organizational dynamics in their entirety. The associate pastor is "pinched" in every direction.

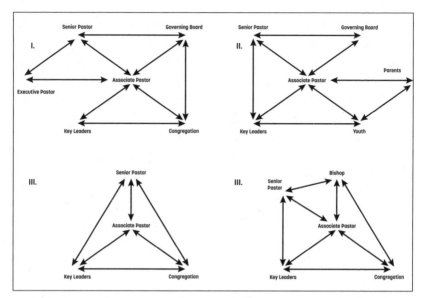

Figure 8-2: Other Associate Pastor Congregational Frameworks

Therefore, while associate pastors often feel the disruptive effects of diffusion in their work, they can have a truly integrative role in their congregations if they negotiate their middle spaces carefully. This chapter aims to make six implications that can assist associate pastors as integrating forces in their congregation, which allow them to be facilitators of learning. First, associate pastors can negotiate anxiety in relational triangles. Second, they can negotiate political power between constituencies in congregations. Third, associate pastors can steward agency in their congregations. Fourth, associate pastors can direct learning for shared convictions by their congregations. Fifth, associate pastors can practice followership to assist their senior pastors. Finally, associate pastors can learn to embrace as management as a legitimate and valuable pastoral practice.

Associate Pastors Navigate Anxiety in Relational Triangles

Chapter 2 introduced a systems theory called Bowen Family Systems; BFS describes family systems as being held together by relationships that manage anxiety between family or system members (Bowen worked primarily with families, but other researchers have applied the theory to congregations). These relationships are bound together by two opposing forces: the individual force and the togetherness force.[8] In order for the relationship partners to grow and operate in a healthy way, they must develop self-differentiation—the ability to be their own selves without being absorbed emotionally by the other participants or disconnecting from the relationships.[9] Anxiety is the greatest threat to self-differentiation. Since two-participant relationships are often unstable, relational participants translate anxiety onto other relational players, forming triangles that can absorb more relational anxiety than simple dyads.[10]

Steinke describes the self-differentiated leader as having "nonanxious presence." Nonanxious presence has several capacities, but two particularly significant ones are the ability to "tolerate high degrees of uncertainty, frustration, and pain," and to "maintain a clear sense of direction."[11] Friedman suggests that a self-differentiated leader has three attributes: he or she stays in touch with the congregation; he or she takes nonreactive and clear positions; and he or she has the capacity to deal with sabotage, or the automatic subconscious reactivity of followers.[12] Nonanxious presence requires emotional intelligence—the ability of a leader to understand emotions "as well as strengths, limitations, values and motives," in order to manage followers well.[13] Similarly, Steinke recommends five practices for regulating anxiety and maintaining nonanxious presence:

1. Knowing your limits and the limits of others
2. Having clarity about what you believe
3. Taking stands with courage
4. Staying on course
5. Staying connected to others[14]

---

8   Kerr and Bowen, *Family Evaluation*, 64–65.
9   Kerr and Bowen, *Family Evaluation*, 94.
10   Kerr and Bowen, *Family Evaluation*, 135.
11   Steinke, *Congregational Leadership in Anxious Times*, 35.
12   Friedman, *Generation to Generation*, 229–30.
13   Burns, Chapman, and Guthrie, *Resilient Ministry*, 103.
14   Steinke, *Congregational Leadership in Anxious Times*, 44–45.

In a congregation with a strong governing board, associate pastors sit in four Bowen triangles, where expectations expressed as role stress in terms of role conflict and role ambiguity have the potential to create emotional anxiety. The best example of role conflict exists between the senior pastor and the key leaders in the congregation. At the key leader or volunteer position, associate pastors were not universally perceived as pastors despite their titles or job descriptions. At the senior pastor position and elder position, associate pastors were seen as pastors. Associate pastors had to negotiate the ambiguity they felt by asserting their authority in the situation without overwhelming their volunteers or disconnecting them.

The associate pastors interviewed demonstrated Steinke's five practices, though some demonstrated greater capacity for nonanxious presence than others. Take the following examples, which highlight each practice: Alex was quite aware of his strengths and would not venture into their areas of weakness. Isaac firmly believed that it was time for his church to be done with camping and focus on another form of children's ministry; this allowed him to take a stand with his elder board about closing the church's camp. Frank was not afraid to take stands with his senior pastor behind closed doors. Becca stayed on course when it came to her volunteers by narrowing the focus on their specific win. Noah was working to take courageous stands with volunteers who didn't want to implement his growth group strategy for missional communities. Colin did a fabulous job of growing relationships with his volunteers.

Associate Pastors Negotiate Political Power Between Constituencies

"Politics" is *the* four-letter-word in congregational circles; but politics is also a necessary part of church life. Mark DeVries suggests that politics is really just relationships working out in the world of the congregation in the give-and-take of daily life.[15] In other words, politics is simply a word for negotiating relationships, and relationships

---

15   Mark DeVries, *Sustainable Youth Ministry*, 176–77.

are a pastor's bread and butter—or really ought to be. Yet, as a key element of leadership and management, most pastors struggle with politics. Burns, Chapman, and Guthrie write:

> Similarly, pastors must learn to navigate the political real-ities of ministry. Yes, *politics* is a dirty word in the church. But ministry nearly always involves working with people, and people have divergent amounts of influence and dif-fering interests. These interests lead them to act in certain ways when confronted with tough decisions.[16]

In a subsequent book Burns, Chapman, and Guthrie state: "In this book, we assume all of life is political—*incorporating the themes of power, interests, negotiation and ethics.*"[17] In a beautifully short definition, they state: "Politics is the art of getting things done with others." Indeed, "All ministry involves politics."[18]

Without a doubt, then, associate pastors are required to be polit-ical actors within their congregations. They must negotiate between different interests and constituencies within their churches. Yet an additional complicating factor is that associate pastors can belong to multiple constituencies within the congregation—establishing anoth-er point of ambiguity that must be clarified if they are to function effectively within their congregational systems. For example, associate pastors can belong to the elder board, belong to the mid-level cohort of associate staff, and belong to various ministry teams, all at the same time. Their multiple places of belonging present certain opportunities and challenges to negotiating politically inside the congregation.

Cervero and Wilson utilize the metaphor of a planning table to describe how political power impacts work that happens in "complex and messy systems" with adult educational objectives. Cervero and Wil-son describe variants that occur at each part of the table: "The variants

---

16   Burns, Chapman, and Guthrie, *Resilient Ministry*, 27–28.
17   Burns, Chapman, and Guthrie, *The Politics of Ministry*, 17 (emphasis added).
18   Burns, Chapman, and Guthrie, *The Politics of Ministry*, 18.

include references to people 'sitting at the table,' 'who is not at the table,' what people 'bring to the table,' and 'putting issues on the table.'"[19] The various participants who are present at the table bring their own complex interests, motivations, and purposes to the tables upon which they wish to take action.[20] Educational programs in organizations are related to the table participants and their use of power.[21]

Associate pastors negotiate educational ministries at their churches through such tables: "Educational programs matter because they create possible futures in the lives of people, organizations, and communities. These judgments can only be made on the ethical commitments that people bring to the planning table about what these possible futures should be and how they can be achieved through education."[22] Participants can bring hidden agendas to the table, and associate pastors must work to conquer their naivety about their own hidden agendas or the hidden agendas of other participants.[23]

Notice, then, that maintaining nonanxious presence while navigating relationships is directly tied to negotiating political power. Each Bowen triangle in a congregation with a governing board is also a negotiating table at which the associate pastor sits. In addition, associate pastors also occupy a negotiation at the middle level with other associate staff. At each table, associate pastors negotiate different elements of their ministry. In the top triangle (the senior pastor, governing board, and associate pastor table), the vision of the organization is discussed and established. The participants at this table are attempting to establish a clear direction for the church. Logan, for example, participated at such a table as voting elder, though it presented awkward tensions between he and his senior pastor.

At the governing board, congregation, and associate pastor table, the participants are negotiating the consensus of the church. Here,

---

19   Cervero and Wilson, *Working the Planning Table,* 6; cf. Burns, Chapman, and Guthrie, *The Politics of Ministry*, 113–14.
20   Cervero and Wilson, *Working the Planning Table,* 88.
21   Cervero and Wilson, *Working the Planning Table,* 89.
22   Cervero and Wilson, *Working the Planning Table,* 91.
23   Cervero and Wilson, *Working the Planning Table,* 90.

the congregation is demonstrating its trust in the leadership as well as its willingness to enact the vision of the church. As an example, remember Irene was triangled in between her board and her congregation over a divisive theological issue, which she handled by backing the board's decision but empathizing with the grievances of the congregation. At the key leader, congregation, and associate pastor table, the participants are negotiating the implementation of the church's vision. Every associate pastor clearly articulated the need to train volunteers to do the work of the ministry so the whole congregation could be fruitful. At the key leader, senior pastor, and associate pastor table, the participants are negotiating the agency of the associate pastor, senior pastor, and key leaders. At the mid-level, the associate pastors and other mid-level staff negotiate alignment by determining how they will collaborate and cooperate with one another to accomplish the tasks in their specific ministries.

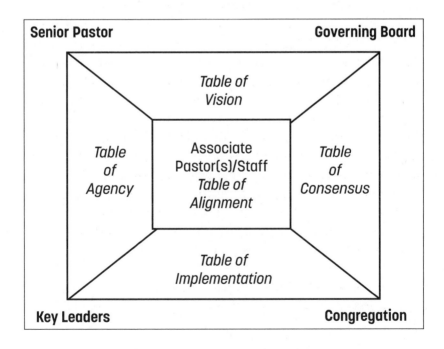

Figure 8-3: The Five Negotiating Tables

It is also important to note that in congregations, not all of the negotiating tables are explicit and formal. While the top triangle between the associate pastor, senior pastor, and elder board certainly sits at a formal and explicit table, and while key leaders and associate pastors on teams may gather at an explicit and formal table to plan ministries, many of the tables at which associate pastors must negotiate are informal and tacit, and occur daily and not merely at formally calendared or appointed times. Hence, associate pastors must negotiate between the power and identity that is sometimes not granted to them by their key leadership volunteers, and the power and identity granted them by the senior pastor. Or, associate pastors must negotiate between the varying perspectives that might occur between the senior pastor and an elder board, or the elder board and the congregation, even if they do not occupy a formal seat on a governing board.

Associate Pastors Steward Agency

Associate pastors described their relationship with their senior pastors and with their key leaders in terms of trust. As we saw in chapter 5, associate pastors looked for a reciprocation of trust between themselves and their senior pastors. Rodin suggests that relationships require mutual reciprocation, which he defines through the lens of presence. Presence is an act of love, where the partners view relationships as ends in themselves, and are viewed as being with people in community.[24] "In community, we are not just individuals but we are interdependent and mutually accountable and trusting."[25]

Associate pastors described trust toward their senior pastors as the development of relationships, open communication, and support for the senior pastor's vision and decision. DeVries writes about trust between youth directors/pastors and their senior pastors:

> Trust is our most valuable currency for dealing with senior leadership. And trust, as we know, takes a long time to build

---

24   Rodin, *The Steward Leader*, 136.
25   Rodin, *The Steward Leader*, 137.

and only seconds to destroy. A single ignored assignment, a single delayed response, a single expression of gossip about the senior pastor to someone else on the church staff, and the value of our currency diminishes exponentially.[26]

In exchange, associate pastors wanted to experience trust with their senior pastors in the form of access, appropriate accountability, and the freedom to be creative in their own ministries. Rodin states, "Only in freedom can a leader allow the room, the ambiguity and the trust necessary for a [kingdom]-oriented culture to emerge."[27] He writes further:

> The steward leader will not deny that people need some sense of order and a set of basic ground rules within that order to operate. However, freedom is a highly prized value, and steward leaders excel in granting it and protecting it.[28]

At the same time, the interviews demonstrated that associate pastors also desired reciprocation of trust with their key leadership volunteers. Particularly, associate pastors wanted their volunteers and congregations to trust them with the direction of the ministry, but associate pastors also wanted to trust volunteers with greater ministry responsibility. Associate pastors felt the need to evaluate their volunteers' ministry abilities but also to give them the requisite freedom and opportunity to shape their ministries. Associate pastors were often frustrated by the lack of relational authority that was sometimes withheld by key volunteers who participated in small groups or held other key roles in congregational life.

As we also saw in chapter 3, Guthrie developed a theory called facilitated agency (FA) in higher education, which may provide a helpful parallel to facilitating learning in a church setting. FA is

---

26 DeVries, *Sustainable Youth Ministry*, 183.
27 Rodin, *The Steward Leader*, 146–47.
28 Rodin, *The Steward Leader*, 147.

theologically rooted in five great callings of the biblical narrative: the
creation mandate, Jesus's invitation to rest in John 15:9, security in
Jesus's lordship, fruitful discipleship, and the Great Commission.[29]

> In light of the five great callings, the core values of FA in-
> clude acknowledging the Triune God as creator, sustainer,
> redeemer, and restorer of all creation, embracing a teach-
> able creational grace perspective that understands all God's
> truth is God's truth; recognizing Christians as fallen but
> redemptively fruitful image bearers; embracing personal and
> corporate Christian formation as a blessing and responsi-
> bility; and cultivating hospitable pedagogy that nurtures a
> gospel-healthy learning climate for all participants.[30]

In FA, the faculty member is a facilitator, the student is a responsible agent in the world, and an iterative process guides inquiry in a
setting described as a learning community, which enriches the total
community and not simply the individual student or professor.[31] If
this theory were applied to a congregational setting, the associate
pastor could find himself or herself as both facilitator and student,
working to provide iterative ministry in the congregation as a learning
community. Under a senior pastor's facilitation, the associate pastor
cooperates to create iterative and responsive ministry. As the facilitator, the associate pastor works to provide an environment where
in a cooperative partnership meaningful ministry enriches the entire
congregation.

Stewarding or facilitating agency is not a condition of a purely
linear process. Figure 8-4 sets the associate pastor's position in a congregation's organizational chart in comparison to a congregational
system's chart. In the linear organizational chart, associate pastors
discover to whom they are directly accountable and report (usually

29 Guthrie, "Facilitated Agency," 163–65.
30 Guthrie, "Facilitated Agency," 165.
31 Guthrie, "Facilitated Agency," 165–68.

the senior pastor), and who is directly accountable and reports to them (the key leaders of the congregation). The organizational chart expresses linear reporting and accountability and gives the impression that a command-and-control management style is in operation in a congregation, particularly in the day-to-day operations between senior pastor, associate pastor, and key leaders.

In contrast, the systems chart displays that relationships and decision-making in congregations are anything but linear; rather, they are always systemic. Associate pastors reciprocate or desire to reciprocate trust with their senior pastors, and key leaders to accomplish pastoral and ministerial responsibilities, rather than enforcing a command-and-control model of leadership, especially in day-to-day operations. Not surprisingly, the negotiating tables described in Figure 8-3 deeply influence the day-to-day operations and relationships that associate pastors experience. In fact, the determination of agency is the task of the negotiating table between the associate pastor, senior pastor, and key leaders.

However, the other tables of vision, consensus, alignment, and implementation also impact the stewardship of agency, since the relationships being developed and the political interests being negotiated influence how the associate pastor will attempt to steward their agency as well as the agency of the senior pastor and key leaders. Associate pastors are responsive politically and relationally to the board and the congregation while they steward the agency of the senior pastor and the volunteers below them. The board will influence how the associate pastor responds to the senior pastor, and the congregation will influence how the associate pastor responds to the key leadership. The relationships throughout are by nature triangled and are not purely linear, though the associate pastor has a more direct impact on the senior pastor and key leadership because of role responsibilities. Stewarding agency is done in the context of negotiating interests.

The associate pastor stewards the agency of the senior pastor by developing relationships, keeping communication open, and supporting his or her vision; the senior pastor facilitates the agency of the associate pastor by granting access, appropriate accountability, and freedom to be creative. The associate pastor stewards the agency of key volunteers by facilitating a narrowing of focus, group discernment, coaching, and spiritual mentorship, all while developing trust and giving appropriate freedom to volunteers; in return, associate pastors hope for trust from their volunteers. The bidirectional arrows in Figure 8-4 signal the interaction of trust between senior pastor and associate pastor and associate pastor and key volunteer. Trust is a primary element in how associate pastors steward the agency of the volunteers and their senior pastors. Without trust, the challenges of fulfilling role responsibilities and facilitating learning become more difficult.

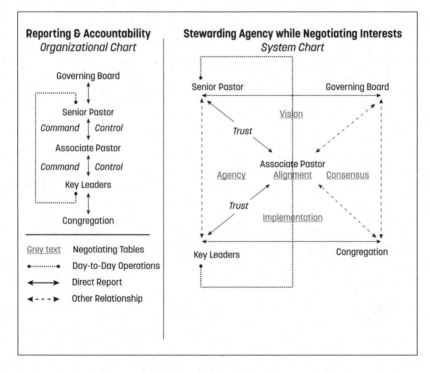

**Figure 8-4: Reporting and Accountability
versus Stewarding Agency**

The themes presented by the associate pastors indicated a number of strategies for facilitating the learning of key leaders, but facilitating learning at the top of the organization was not discussed widely. In terms of the chart, while reciprocating trust ensured agency throughout the structure, facilitating of learning for associate pastors almost exclusively occurred in the bottom triangle of the framework.

Associate Pastors Direct Learning for Shared Convictions

Now, what about learning and education? Associate pastors spend much of their time and energy organizing learning in the congregation, and that learning extends in two directions: their own personal learning, and the learning of the congregational members. As a brief reminder, I've reproduced the table from chapter 7 that describes practices associate pastors use for facilitating learning in their congregations.

Table 8-1: Associate Pastor Strategies for Facilitating Learning

Utilize Orientation Points	Manage Tensions	Practices
Biblical Texts	Ministry Within versus Outside the Congregation	Narrow the Focus
Congregational Vision	Centralized versus Decentralized Ministry	Gathering Groups to Set Direction
Picture of a Mature Disciple	Sunday school versus Small Groups	Coaching Key Leaders
	Content versus Practice	Acting as a Spiritual Mentor

Associate pastors work to reorient their congregations toward Scripture, the vision of the congregation, or a shared understanding of a mature disciple. As associate pastors utilize these orientation points, they are faced with organizational tensions that express the pull between being inwardly or outwardly focused (Jenna's healing versus missional, John's institutional versus missional, Paul's centralized versus decentralized). They face a limited amount of contact time with their congregation, and attempt to choose between various modes of education (usually expressed in Sunday morning education or small groups during the week).

As associate pastors face these tensions, they face their own need for learning in theology and management. While associate pastors were generally very good about discovering their own needs—both in staying calm and managing anxiety, and in developing necessary skills for pastoral practice—they often struggled or expressed frustration that there wasn't an intentional agenda for learning in the congregation. Associate pastors paid specific attention to creating opportunities to mentor specific leaders and coach critical volunteers. Some were adept at developing groups for discerning ways forward for their ministries and setting educational agendas.

Critical to the task of organizational learning is the facilitator's ability to create educational systems that allow a transfer of ideas and beliefs. If there was a place where associate pastors struggled with intentionality, it was in this specific arena. This is not to say that associate pastors did not set up educational ministries or platforms; indeed, creating educational ministries often made up the bulk of their work. However, the challenge of reorienting the whole of the congregation to a new direction was a recurring struggle for many of the associate pastors interviewed.

Associate pastors were adept at organizing their own learning from multiple sources and for multiple reasons, both interior to and exterior from the congregation (Figure 8-5). However, when they described their learning and how they taught others, associate pastors organized their educational efforts at the bottom portion of the congregation, rather than at the congregation's top, and relied on informal learning with their senior pastors and board members (Figure 8-6).

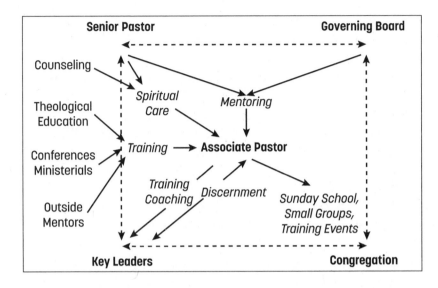

Figure 8-5: How Associate Pastors Learn and Teach

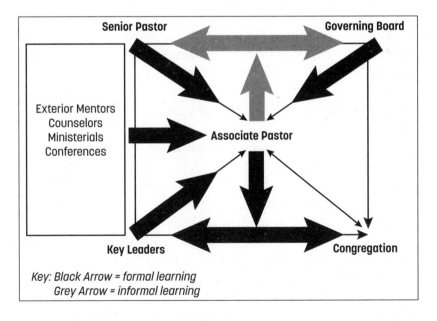

Figure 8-6: How Learning Spreads Through Associate Pastors

Facilitators of learning diffuse learning and knowledge throughout the entirety of an organization. This requires the facilitator of learning to examine their experiences and reflect on them critically. It would appear that for associate pastors, critical reflection happens in the mentoring relationships from above and below them in the organization, as well as those they have outside the organization. Associate pastors learn how to act within the organization primarily from their own reading and research as well as from learning outside the organization. In terms of diffusing learning in the organization, associate pastors put their skills into practice through the creation of formal vehicles for learning such as small groups, Sunday school classes, and formal training and mentoring.

The absence of formal mechanisms at the top of the congregation does not mean associate pastors did not diffuse learning to the top of the organization. While the learning was presented in formal educational challenges to key leaders and the congregation as a whole, associate pastors diffused learning via informal means at the top of the organization. This sort of learning happens in negotiations behind closed doors, informal planning sessions, and at board meetings, which are perceived of as political rather than educational venues. What is ironic about this arrangement is that while associate pastors are perceived as pastors at the "top" of the congregational structure and have their pastoral status contested at the bottom of the organization, they rely heavily on formal education at the bottom of the organization.

Can associate pastors create more formal avenues for learning at the top? This task seems largely in the control of their senior pastors; indeed, associate pastors can have ambiguous interactions and relationships with board members, though associate pastors may have board members function as key leaders in their ministry, in which case board members participate in the more formal educational structures of the church. But associate pastors typically rely on negotiation and relationship to diffuse learning at the top. This requires them to put into practice another vital skill: followership.

Associate Pastors and Followership

Associate pastors, as subordinates of their senior pastors, are well aware of the asymmetrical power relationship present between them and their senior pastors. Associate pastors recognized that the "buck stopped" with the senior pastor, and recognized their responsibility to support the vision and ministry of the senior pastor.

Associate pastors saw the senior pastor as the primary vision-caster of the congregation. Associate pastors also expressed frustration and concern when senior pastors either abdicated their role as vision-caster or did not cast a clear vision to the congregation. Abdication of the role of vision-caster put associate pastors in the anxiety-producing tension of either waiting for the senior pastor to cast a vision or stepping into the role of vision-casting themselves.

Chaleef describes the relationship between leader and follower as mutual revolution around a common purpose. While the leader is responsible for stewarding the communication and implementation of the vision, the follower is also responsible for being loyal to the vision, which is distinct from the leader. Without clear purpose, "leader and followers can only pursue their perceived self-interest, not the common interest."[32] Many associate pastors in this study felt flummoxed about the vision or lack thereof projected by their senior pastors. When lack of vision was present, followership for the associate pastor was not a mutual orbit around a vision but an orbit around the senior pastor.

Figure 8-7 illustrates the difference between Chaleef's framework and the reality articulated by many associate pastors in the study. In Diagram 1, Chaleef's model of followership is presented. Diagram 2 presents the senior pastor/associate pastor model as it would function if it matched Chaleef's model.

Becca's relationship to her SP best reflects Diagram 2. Her pastor discerned the need for a ministry to reach out to young adults in their context, and both she and he orbited around developing such a ministry. In Diagram 3, the purpose of the congregation is not clearly

---

32   Chaleef, *The Courageous Follower*, 13.

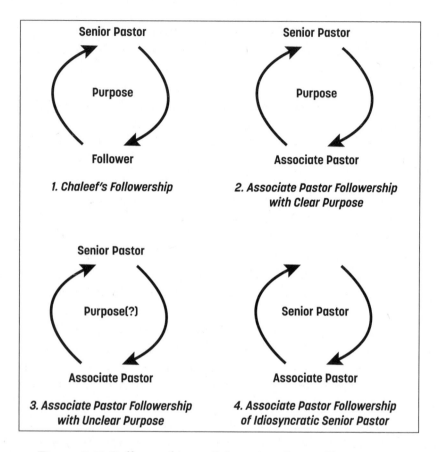

Figure 8-7: Followership and Associate Pastor Experiences

communicated, and there is ambiguity about the responsibility for developing a vision or purpose for the congregation. Noah found himself in such a situation, when his senior pastor did not take responsibility for articulating a clear vision. His senior pastor simply allowed Noah to implement his own vision for missional communities.

In Diagram 4, there is no vision at all, and the associate pastor simply orbits the idiosyncrasies of his or her senior pastor. Amy's senior pastor cast vision after vision, but never produced a cohesive purpose for the church. As a result, Amy and her fellow associates simply orbited around his most recent idea.

Chaleef remarks that followers serve two organizational entities: the members or clients it exists to serve, and its leaders.[33] While serving dual constituencies is meant to occur without conflict of interest, Chaleef notes seven paradoxes that associate pastors certainly experience. Followers must have:

1. a clear internal vision of service while being attached to a leader who embodies that vision externally.
2. accountability for their actions while relinquishing autonomy and conceding authority.
3. a willingness to be both implementer and challenger of their leader's vision.
4. a willingness to exist in tension of dual identity as group member and challenger of the group and its leadership.
5. a willingness to be mentored by the leader and to challenge the leader.
6. an ability to sustain the leader's vision or the leader.
7. an ability to act as leader and follower at the same time.[34]

Associate pastors demonstrated some of these tensions. Micah exhibited the first tension quite clearly. He attached himself to his senior pastor because of the senior pastor's external embodiment of love for their community. Alex, Frank, and Logan were exemplars of being both implementer and challenger of their senior pastors' positions. Alex particularly could identify with a dual identity as devil's advocate but also group member by falling in line when a decision was made. Associate pastors were certainly able to act as leaders and followers by the very nature of their positions. Becca for example, led the new initiative to reach out to young adults in her community, but she was implementing her senior pastor's vision.

An additional complicating factor in the tension between subordinate and partner is the tension between professional relationship

---

33   Chaleef, *The Courageous Follower*, 15.
34   Chaleef, *The Courageous Follower*, 44–45.

and personal relationship. While some associate pastors functioned comfortably with "warm enough" or "distant" relationships, some were close friends with their senior pastors, desired closer friendships, or wanted more intentional mentoring.

Conversely, associate pastors occupy the leadership role in follower relationships with their key volunteers. In such a role, associate pastors can experience pressure from the bottom when there is no vision for the congregation or for a ministry, when key volunteers do not share the vision for the congregation or ministry, or when the associate pastor feels pressure to capitulate to a volunteer's vision for the ministry.

Management as a Pastoral Practice

"In order for pastors to thrive in ministry, they must accept the fact that they are leaders and managers";[35] yet seminary and formal ministerial training rarely prepare pastors for these two skills.[36] Left to develop them on the job, associate pastors spent a significant portion of the facilitation of their own learning developing skills as managers and administrators of people and resources. Often acknowledging that they received training at the seminary level for understanding, teaching, and preaching the Bible, they felt ill at ease and often surprised at the amount of managerial responsibilities that fell to them as associate pastors.

Management requires associate pastors to do quite a bit of oversight of their key leaders and can be as diverse as teaching biblical study skills, making sure they are equipped with necessary supplies and resources, or engaging in counseling and spiritual direction or formation.

Block prefers the concept of stewardship to management. He describes stewardship as a "willingness to be accountable for results without using control or caretaking as the means to reach them."[37] Stewardship is accountability for the outcomes through the orderly dispersion of power to the bottoms and edges of organizations.[38]

---

35   Burns, Chapman, and Guthrie, *Resilient Ministry*, 26.
36   Burns, Chapman, and Guthrie, *Resilient Ministry*, 26.
37   Block, *Stewardship*, 58.
38   Block, *Stewardship*, 27.

Block sees stewardship as inherently spiritual, which he describes as the process of living out of a set of deeply held personal values, of honoring force or a presence greater than ourselves: "To honor the spirit, patriarchy must be replaced by partnership, and accountability must be separated from control, consistency, and predictability."[39]

Stewardship of individuals and resources is a biblical theme throughout Scripture. Wilson compares modern management with Greco-Roman stewardship. Stewards must be well trained and be willing to continue learning. They must not be sexually indulgent while being good examples to their servants or employees. They must motivate others with proper rewards without expectation of being served.[40]

Jesus taught that servanthood and leadership are inherently tied together (Matt. 20:24–28) and that leadership in the kingdom of God is not described by dominance. Scazzero links decision-making and church leadership to power, which he describes as the capacity to influence, and notes that many leaders have little personal awareness of power or how to use it responsibly. Scazzero suggests that, following Jesus's teaching in Matthew 20:25, the proper stewardship of power is seen in the service of others. Rather than exercising power over other organizational partners, leaders can use "power under" strategy that serves others in the organization. Scazzero is intentional in his choice of the word "stewardship": "We must never forget that the power we exercise belongs to [God]. Our power is given to us to come under people for their good, for them to flourish, not so we will look good."[41]

Nonetheless, associate pastors lamented that management seemed to them relegated to on-the-job learning, or what one associate pastor referred to as trial by fire. Management was described as often learned through reading, attending conferences, or through one-on-one coaching with external mentors, as opposed

---

39   Block, *Stewardship*, 31, 51, 57, 59; cf. Ritzer, *The McDonaldization of Society.*
40   Wilson, *Steward Leadership in the Nonprofit Organization*, 44–47.
41   Scazzero, *The Emotionally Healthy Leader*, 242, 243, 254–55.

to studied in seminary or other theological institutions. Associate pastors did not naturally view management through theological or biblical lenses, and often did not possess management strategies for managing people or projects. Yet associate pastors did identify their roles strongly with management and spent a large amount of time supervising and training others, often through the dominant strategies of one-on-one coaching but occasionally by gathering key leaders together to set direction in a larger group. Sometimes one-on-one coaching depended on defining the win or narrowing the focus so that volunteers were able to stay true to the church's vision and have clarity about expectations. One-on-one coaching often involved forms of negotiation between the interests of a key volunteer and the interests of the associate pastor or those above him or her. The negotiation often included defining objectives and ensuring adequate oversight and accountability without overwhelming the freedom of the volunteer.

There are a variety of tools available for associate pastors to assist them with their tasks as stewards or managers. As was briefly discussed, critical reflection, negotiation and dialogue are forms of such tools. If associate pastors could develop a greater appreciation for management as a pastoral practice, these tools could be powerful ways of unifying congregations to a common vision under the headship of Jesus.

It is important to see the six implications of this chapter interacting systemically with one another, and not merely as standalone points. The ministry of associate pastors is the confluence of a system of related dynamics that flow out of the middleness of their positions.

Figure 8-8 describes the systemic nature of the implications. The six implications are all in interaction with one another and influence each other. They are not arranged in a particular order, though all flow out of management as a pastoral practice. The diagram simply illustrates that management, Bowen triangles, negotiating political power, enacting followership, and stewarding agency all influence each other in a nonlinear, non-cause-and-effect manner. To act out one of the implications is to act out all of the others.

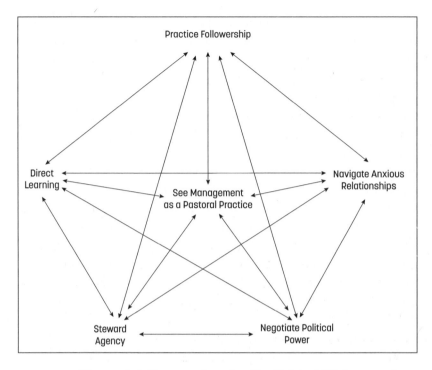

Figure 8-8: Integrating the Six Critical Tasks

For example, associate pastors experience the tension of negotiating political power between the participants in the congregation in Bowen family triangles, such as when an associate pastor is caught between a key leader suggesting that he or she is not a real pastor and a senior pastor insisting that he or she has been hired to be a pastor, or he or she is caught in the middle of an emotional triangle as well as a political negotiation. In addition, followership systemically interacts with political negotiation and stewarding agency. The associate pastor must clarify the vision and mission of the church as a political actor while demonstrating trust and executing a proper followership dynamic with the senior pastor by supporting decisions and staying in communication.

As a further example, management, when described as serving others, interacts with followership and the stewardship of agency.

When an associate pastor serves a key leader by coaching or giving them the trust required to perform their ministries, the associate pastor is stewarding the agency of the volunteer but is also serving as a follower by implementing the purpose or the vision of the congregation. The associate pastor is also functioning in a Bowen triangle, as he or she assists the key leader in ministering to the congregation. In short, an associate pastor, when he or she is doing any one of the implications of this study, is likely doing all of them at the same time.

The Big Takeaway

It may be helpful to realize that for centuries, even some of the greatest examples of Christian leadership were reluctant to take up ministry positions precisely because handling relationships was indeed so difficult. St. John Chrysostom, in his book on pastoral duties, wrote: "I know how weak and puny my own soul is. I know the importance of [pastoral] ministry and the great difficulty of it. More billows toss the priest's soul than the gales which trouble the sea."[42] Part III of St. Gregory the Great's *The Pastoral Rule* is given over to assisting different groups of people under a pastor's care. Each group of people is divided into two subgroups (e.g., men and women, young and old, poor and rich). St. Gregory begins each section with the phrase, "Therefore, [the first group] is to be advised one way and [the second group] another."[43] Clearly, relationships are complicated in churches and congregations; they always have been and always will be. Associate pastors cannot use the excuse of complicated relationships to avoid their responsibilities as pastors.

The most important skill associate pastors require is the ability to navigate complicated relationships and to understand the navigation of these relationships as a pastoral practice. Training in relational dynamics might ease tensions as associate pastors enter their role, since relational dynamics are the essential factors that

---

42   St. John Chyrsostom, *Six Books of the Priesthood*, 77.
43   St. Gregory the Great, *The Book of Pastoral Rule*, 88, 90–91.

associate pastors must navigate as they minister within the congregation, particularly as they coach volunteers and leaders or gather others to discern direction and vision. Learning then occurs in the matrix of relationships, as associate pastors try to clarify or create vision and orient practice of vision and mission through a variety of orientation points and practices.

For example, Farrah, a worship pastor, aligned all of her key volunteers to an explicit theology of worship that guided the congregational worship times. The senior pastor had clearly laid out expectations, and Farrah had access to him, but Farrah was responsible for implementing the vision—the theology of worship—into the services, and had the freedom to do so as creatively as necessary. By coaching her key volunteers, she empowered them to lead the whole congregation into worship. Farrah, negotiating worship between the worship leaders and the congregation, and the worship leaders and the senior pastor, facilitated learning within the web of the relationships.

Alex received a clear set of principles from the senior pastor and elders that he was required to implement in his youth ministry. However, he was given clear parameters and freedom as to how he could implement the principles. While he enforced the principles, he gave a maximum amount of freedom to his volunteers to perform their ministry according to their gifts, while he coached them on following the principles. When principles were unclear, Alex had the flexibility to push back on the senior pastor's vision until a decision was made or clarity was reached. Alex could influence the learning both up and down the organization, through the triangle of the senior pastor and the elders to the key volunteers and his youth group.

Repentance as a Spiritual Discipline for Personal Learning

"Repent!" Jesus called out, "for the kingdom of heaven is at hand!" (Matt. 4:17). What does repentance look like, and how indeed does it facilitate relationships? Repentance is, of course, more than the mere knowledge of personal sin and the ability to say that one is sorry. Rather, repentance is a total change of the person—a conversion of the person.

> I appeal to you therefore, brothers, by the mercies of God, to present your bodies as a living sacrifice, holy and acceptable to God, which is your spiritual worship. Do not be conformed to this world, but be transformed by the renewal of your mind, that by testing you may discern what is the will of God, what is good and acceptable and perfect. (Rom. 12:1–2)

It is worth noting that Paul's admonition to conversion in verses 1–2 of Romans 12 comes before verse 3, where Christians are to individually evaluate themselves "with sober judgment, each according to the measure of faith that God has assigned," and before verses 4–8, where all Christians are to see themselves as a part of a unified body, with whom they must coordinate their gifts, "members one of another" (12:5).

In the Sermon on the Mount, repentance is seen as a radical righteousness. While all Christians together are the light of the world and the salt of the earth, they are also to watch their actions carefully in order to demonstrate a righteousness that reflects the kingdom of God (Matt. 5:13–16). Christians, unlike Cain in Genesis 4, are to hold anger in check and seek out reconciliation with those they have wronged; are to hold sexual desire in check and hold to fidelity to one's spouse; are to hold to the truth regardless of circumstance; and are to renounce revenge and love their enemies (5:21–48).

It is wise to understand one's ability to understand one's anxiety as a part of rejecting the pattern of the world and conforming to the pattern of Christ and his kingdom. Jesus encourages his disciples not to be anxious over what they will eat or wear, and Paul does the same in his letters (Matt. 6:25–34; Phil. 4:5–6).

Henri Nouwen directly confronts the contours of modern leadership. He suggests three temptations derived from the story of Jesus's temptation, each of which arise from pastoral anxieties and which pastoral leaders need to constantly face and reject: the temptations to be relevant,[44] spectacular or popular,[45] and pow-

---

44 Nouwen, *In the Name of Jesus*, 15.
45 Nouwen, *In the Name of Jesus*, 35.

erful.[46] Each temptation is paired with an insight derived from Jesus's recommissioning of Peter at the end of John: the challenge to love Christ and our churches;[47] the challenge to see ministry as communal and mutual experience, which puts the pastor in close relationship with the community;[48] and the challenge to be led rather than to lead.[49]

Scazzero suggests that facing one's shadow is essential to healthy ministry: "Your shadow is the accumulation of untamed emotions, less-than-pure motives and that, while largely unconscious, strongly influence your shape and your behaviors. It is the damaged but mostly hidden version of who you are."[50] The shadow can manifest as sinful behavior, negative emotions, and through the pastor's needs: "a need to rescue others and be liked by other people, a need to be noticed, an inability to stop working, a tendency toward isolation and rigidity."[51] To ignore one's shadow is to undermine our ability to be our best,[52] limit our ability to serve,[53] and blind us to others' shadows.[54] Scazzero suggests four paths to face the shadow:

1. Taming your feelings by naming your feelings
2. Using a genogram to explore the impact of your past
3. Identifying negative scripts handed down to you
4. Seeking feedback from trustworthy sources[55]

Both Nouwen's and Scazzero's advice require learning from others. Submission to the truth requires walking after Jesus in a wise matter in dark, evil, and thus anxious times (Eph. 5:15), as we imitate

---

46 Nouwen, *In the Name of Jesus*, 55.
47 Nouwen, *In the Name of Jesus*, 23.
48 Nouwen, *In the Name of Jesus*, 42–43.
49 Nouwen, *In the Name of Jesus*, 46.
50 Scazzero, *The Emotionally Healthy Leader*, 55.
51 Scazzero, *The Emotionally Healthy Leader*, 55.
52 Scazzero, *The Emotionally Healthy Leader*, 61.
53 Scazzero, *The Emotionally Healthy Leader*, 63.
54 Scazzero, *The Emotionally Healthy Leader*, 65.
55 Scazzero, *The Emotionally Healthy Leader*, 70–80.

Christ's love (5:1–2) and as we are filled with the Spirit (5:18). This Spirit-provided wisdom comes through mutual submission to others (5:21). Learning is thus an act of submission to Christ through the Spirit's wisdom given to his people. Only then is transformation possible, for the associate pastor *and* for the congregation. As Elmer and Elmer remind us, by being surrounded by the priesthood of all believers we can confront the changes necessary in our lives to embody the gospel in the ministry of our congregations.[56]

Discernment as a Critical Skill for Congregational Learning

While pastors may be the ultimate implementers of decisions that resolve ambiguity, and while they may be the moderators of any attempt to discover ways forward in ambiguity, the weight of thinking through decisions is too great for any one particular agent to bear. Van Gelder, in his analysis of Romans 12:1–2, reminds us that while the subjects of the verses are all plural, the objects are singular. Paul commands, in view of God's mercy, that the church in Rome present their bodies as a single living sacrifice, in a single act of worship, that they share a common mind through which they are able to discern the will of God. "Paul is inviting the Roman congregation to understand its unity in the midst of its diversity. . . . In this way, they are better able to come to an understanding of the will of God, both that which is revealed generally in Scripture that which is communally discerned and agreed to by a congregation within a specific context."[57] Branson and Martínez help us frame this idea in the context of congregational learning through praxis: "All the work of practical theology—the repeating cycle of praxis-theory-praxis—is processed through relationships."[58]

Branson and Martínez suggest decision-making in congregations requires interpretive, relational, and implemental leadership:[59] "Each

---

56 Elmer and Elmer, *The Learning Cycle*, 143.
57 Van Gelder, *The Ministry of the Missional Church*, 114–15.
58 Branson and Martínez, *Churches, Cultures, and Leadership*, 56.
59 Branson and Martínez, *Churches, Cultures, and Leadership*, 212–13.

sphere requires we perceive, interpret, and act concerning on-the-ground situations."[60] The interpretive task binds the relational and the implemental tasks together as the integrating factor in the triad: "If they lose their cohesion, then organizational dysfunction results."[61]

Surely associate pastors sit in the very nexus of such an interpretive, relational, and implemental triad. Associate pastors are called to interpret the ambiguity and possibilities of ministry in the middle of an organization within diverse relationships and then assist in the implementation of solutions to the ambiguity. If a single spiritual practice could be named to describe this particular responsibility, it would be discernment.

We briefly discussed negotiation, dialogue, critical reflection, and discernment as significant tools for facilitating learning, as well as important tools for associate pastors in negotiating political tensions. All these forms of communication are intensely relational. For example, Fisher, Ury, and Patton[62] suggest that negotiators remember that table partners are interested in relationships as well as the substance or issue being negotiated. Thus, negotiators identify *common interests rather than fight about specific interests*, while inventing options for mutual gain. Likewise Schwarz[63] reminds the facilitative learner that all participants in negotiation have relevant information, may see things others don't, might be contributors to the problem while not seeing it, and present differences that are opportunities for learning. Scharmer and Kaufer's concept of presencing[64] is a process which depends on the suspension of past behaviors and beliefs, so that new beliefs and behaviors can guide the organization into a preferred future. Isaacs's[65] model of dialogue describes a conversation where participants dissolve problems "to create a context from which many new agreements might come."

---

60   Branson and Martínez, *Churches, Cultures, and Leadership*, 55.
61   Branson and Martínez, *Churches, Cultures, and Leadership*, 55.
62   Fisher, Ury, and Patton, *Getting to Yes*, 9–14.
63   Schwarz, *The Skilled Facilitator*, 88–89.
64   Scharmer and Kaufer, *Leading from the Emerging Future*, 21–22.
65   Isaacs, *Dialogue and the Art of Thinking Together*, 19.

What makes discernment different is that it is a Christian practice, where a moderator leads the congregation to seek the Holy Spirit's guidance. Discernment is an ever-increasing capacity to "see or discern the works of God in the midst of the human situation so that we can align ourselves with whatever God is doing. . . . *Discernment together as leaders* takes us beyond the personal to an increasing capacity to 'see' what God is up to in the place we are called to lead."[66]

Guder writes, "Missional communities witness to the nature and quality of God's presence in their midst through worship and their service. But they also witness just as strongly in the way they share power and influence in their decision making."[67] Writing further, he states:

> Discernment is a process of sorting, distinguishing, evaluating, and sifting among competing stimuli, demands, longings, desires, needs, and influences, in order to determine which are of God and which are not. To discern is to prove or test "what is of the will of God—what is good and acceptable and perfect" (Rom. 12:2). Thus the goal of decision making in the church is not simply to discover the will of the community, but instead to discern together the will of God.[68]

Guder suggests that missional communities are neither hierarchical nor egalitarian [that is, democratic], but rather Spirit-led.[69] Thus, congregational leaders must recognize the role of the Holy Spirit in all the congregation; congregations are *pneumocratic*.[70] The leadership thus serves the Holy Spirit and the community in the process of discernment: "it provides the distinctive gifts of biblical and theological insight needed for that discernment. But it is not the exclusive agency of the Spirit within the community." As methods for discernment,

---

66   Barton, *Pursuing God's Will Together*, 20 (emphasis in original).
67   Guder, *Missional Church*, 172.
68   Guder, *Missional Church*, 172.
69   Guder, *Missional Church*, 173.
70   Guder, *Missional Church*, 174.

Guder suggests open dialogue and critical reflection, done in an environment of "genuine respect, mutual trust, and active collaboration."[71] To use language that we've been using in this book, those negotiating with one another will reciprocate trust as they manage their anxiety and their power to make decisions in the wisdom of the Holy Spirit.

Van Gelder suggests that discernment happens at the intersection of the biblical text, context, and community with strategy and action. "The argument presented here is that Christian leaders can mostly effectively lead in mission in Christian congregations by integrating these four dimensions *into a shared process* and by understanding the hermeneutical [that is, interpretative] nature of this process."[72] Van Gelder agrees that such a process is Spirit-led, but also emphasizes the communal nature of discernment: "Leading in mission from a hermeneutical perspective involves a gathered Christian community, with the congregation being the most common public and organized expression as such."[73]

Models of Discernment

Single Learning Loop Models of Discernment

Van Gelder recommends a five-step discernment process that pays attention to the congregational context in light of a specific problem addressing the congregation and its context.

1. Attending: Attention to the congregation's internal and external or cultural context
2. Asserting: Testing alternative strategic choices for action
3. Agreeing: Coming to communally concerned agreement on the strategic point of action in light of biblical/theological concerns
4. Acting: Implementation of the strategic choice
5. Assessing: A thorough review of the implementation process[74]

---

71 Guder, *Missional Church*, 175.
72 Van Gelder, *The Ministry of the Missional Church*, 106 (emphasis added).
73 Van Gelder, *The Ministry of the Missional Church*, 106.
74 Van Gelder, *The Ministry of the Missional Church*, 116–20.

In this contextual model, the congregation is enjoined to pay attention to two significant questions: "What is God doing?" and "What does God want to do?" The first question involves faith and discernment, and the second involves wisdom and planning.[75] Because Van Gelder's process focuses on a strategic change and does not impose a revision of theological convictions or biblical understanding, it appears to be a form of single-loop learning. The congregation addresses significant instrumental changes that do not require a revision of values.

Second and Third Learning Loop Discernment Practice

Branson and Martínez developed a five-step process for discernment. While Van Gelder began with attention to the congregational context, Branson and Martínez begin with the congregation's current praxis (interaction of theological theory and ministerial practice) when addressing a specific problem.[76]

1. Name and describe your current praxis concerning some aspect of church life.
2. Analyze your praxis, seeking to understand all of the influences and consequences, by using resources from your culture.
3. Study and reflect on Scripture, theology and Christian history concerning your praxis and analysis.
4. Recall and discuss stories from your church's history and your own personal lives that are related to the topic under discussion.
5. Corporately discern and shape your new praxis by working with the results of steps 1–4, and then prayerfully naming what you believe to be your priorities.[77]

In this model, the congregation's experience serves as an important entry point into the analysis of the praxis to address a problem: "It is

---

75 Van Gelder, *The Ministry of the Missional Church*, 116–17.
76 Branson and Martínez, *Churches, Cultures, and Leadership*, 42–43.
77 Martínez, *Churches, Cultures, and Leadership*, 43–45.

important to realize that no church enters this work as a blank slate. As is emphasized by the practical theology cycle, a church already has experiences and traditions how they read (or misread) Scripture, what theological perspectives they claim, and how those affirmations shape (or fail to shape) their current practices."[78] In other words, this cycle of discernment forces a church to relate its experience both to its theological claims and to its reading of Scripture. Learning is then pushed into a secondary and tertiary learning loop.

The Associate Pastor's Role in Facilitating Learning Through Discernment

Barton's model of discernment has three phases: preparation, putting the group in a position to lead, and discerning God's will together. Preparation clarifies the specific question on the table and gathers the community for participation according to its values and principles. The second phase is punctuated by prayers for indifference, wisdom, and trust. The third phase is punctuated by listening, silence (which creates space for God to work), and then decision-making.[79] Barton describes different facilitators in discernment processes such as convener,[80] "discernmentarian,"[81] sage,[82] and intercessor.[83] Such leaders need to be self-differentiated and nonanxious,[84] have the trust of the group,[85] be able to sense and verbalize how the Spirit is leading the group,[86] contribute wisdom to the process, or pray for the group.[87] Discernment requires gathering a group from among those being affected by the decision, have relevant experience or special expertise, and who then must implement the decision.[88] The decision is made

---

78   Martínez, *Churches, Cultures, and Leadership*, 44–45.
79   Barton, *Pursuing God's Will Together*, 172.
80   Barton, *Pursuing God's Will Together*, 178.
81   Barton, *Pursuing God's Will Together*, 179.
82   Barton, *Pursuing God's Will Together*, 178–81.
83   Barton, *Pursuing God's Will Together*, 181.
84   Barton, *Pursuing God's Will Together*, 180.
85   Barton, *Pursuing God's Will Together*, 179.
86   Barton, *Pursuing God's Will Together*, 179.
87   Barton, *Pursuing God's Will Together*, 181–82.
88   Barton, *Pursuing God's Will Together*, 183.

in an atmosphere of "indifference," so that the group is led by Christ and not by the specific vision of any particular participant. In this context, indifference is a gift of the Holy Spirit "which is given for the holy purpose of being open to a new work of God."[89]

Conclusion

If associate pastor roles are defined by middleness in the midst of ambiguity, then there are important elements to their ministry that must not be ignored. First, associate pastors are negotiators and political agents within their pastoral roles. Negotiation impacts how associate pastors manage the congregation and facilitate the learning of other participants in the congregation, but associate pastors felt frustrated that much of management, administration, and people skills had to be learned "on the job," rather than being prepared for such tasks in their theological education. Associate pastors have to inhabit their pastoral roles as political negotiators in a way that honors the image of God, the presence and work of the Holy Spirit, and the natural and supernatural talents and abilities in all congregational members.

Second, associate pastors require an additional set of educational skills other than preaching and teaching. Associate pastors felt well prepared in their seminary training to study, preach, and teach the Bible, but felt ill-equipped to manage and interact in complex relational dynamics. The felt inadequacy of associate pastors suggests that seminaries and Christian higher education could expand the curriculum to incorporate relational skill training as a core portion of their curriculum. In other words, while biblical studies and theological training are essential, critical, and fundamental elements of pastoral training, they are insufficient in pastoral preparation. Associate pastors must also be prepared to navigate ambiguous and complex relationships, with skills and practices rooted and biblical and pastoral theology that facilitate learning and agency in the congregation. The skill of negotiating relationships is what will set the fruitful associate pastor apart from those who are struggling in their congregational systems.

---

89   Barton, *Pursuing God's Will Together*, 189.

Coaching and facilitating group direction-setting are key elements of how associate pastors develop agency with key leaders and congregational participants. Such leadership skills are also learned on the job rather than in the theological higher education setting. Associate pastors spend energy and time pursuing learning opportunities in reading, conferences, and mentoring to acquire such skills. Mastering these skills is pivotal to their effectiveness and fruitfulness. Theological education would perform a helpful task to associate pastors in seeing coaching and facilitating groups as an important pastoral task worthy of both theological weight and practical training. But coaching and training should accompany and be supported by the significant Spirit-led task of discernment, which associate pastors are uniquely positioned to carry out due to their being placed in the very center of the congregation as its relational hub.

As we've come to the end of this book describing associate pastor ministry, we can see that associate ministry does offer a unique ministry role for this pinched set of pastors. With the pinched pressure comes great possibilities to hear, understand, teach, and guide the whole congregation as they participate with the Holy Spirit and the remainder of the congregation. This work is highly relational, done in the context of a ministering congregation, and fully deserves to be considered ministry. Those in the middle should be equipped for the specific work of this place and should be equipped and supported to carry it out in their congregations. It was a privilege to serve as an associate pastor, and I would consider doing it again. It is true pastoral work. Let us view it as such.

Preparing Students for Associate Ministry

I think my professor's words, "Be prepared for your first ministry position" have haunted my entire ministerial and academic career. Relationships are the place where theology comes alive. Associate pastors sit at the center of the complicated and messy relationships where the Holy Spirit lives and gives life to the congregation. Since ministry is pneumocratic, as Guder suggests,[1] ministry works to discern how the Holy Spirit is moving in relationships and circumstances in congregations. Associate pastors must be masters of relationships, caring shepherds who empower ministry and navigate complexity and the ambiguity it causes. In these relationships, they work to discern how the Holy Spirit is moving the congregation.

How do you prepare for your first role as an associate pastor? As a professor of Christian ministry, I am an advocate of both undergraduate and graduate preparation for pastors. Yet I also know that the demands on the curriculum of both undergraduate and graduate programs is immense. Greek, Hebrew, systematic theology, hermeneutics, counseling, preaching and liturgy, church polity, missiology and evangelism, ethics, and education all vie for attention and place in a three-to-four-year degree for Master of Divinity students. Many schools provide leadership classes as electives in their ministry program, but I am advocating that unless seminaries train for congre-

---

1   Guder, *Missional Church*, 74.

gational dynamics, many future associate pastors will be ill-prepared for their first positions.

In my ten years of ministry experience, I rarely saw or heard of colleagues and acquaintances being fired from a ministry for teaching or presenting heresy or false doctrine in a congregation, or who had to navigate their churches through the fallout of a senior pastor or other key leader's heresy, though some voluntarily moved on from ministry or pastoring because of changes in their beliefs or convictions. But I can think of many friends, acquaintances, and colleagues who have moved on or left ministry over relational problems in their churches that impacted their ability to do their ministerial tasks.

As I was working on this afterword, a friend who accepted a role as director of children's ministry was let go from her church because her senior pastor mismanaged expectations and created massive ambiguity for her. Another friend shared how his former associate pastor was let go abruptly in a confusing relational situation back at his home church. While explicitly stated heresy and doctrinal error played no role in either situation, in both situations the trouble centered on relational problems where doctrine was misapplied or misunderstood in the context of the relationships. In other words, I think it is likely that doctrine was misapplied in the relationship between senior pastor and associate in some way, shape, or form. To put it another way, the explicit doctrine of the church (the espoused theory) was sound and well communicated from pulpit and pastors, but the day-to-day practice of that theology in the relationships of the congregation (the theory-in-use) was broken and perhaps betrayed the explicit theological convictions of the congregation.

I want to state clearly, as I hope chapter 1 of this book demonstrates, that I am absolutely for doctrinal competency. Pastors are theologians. They should operate as such. Nonetheless, pastors are also shepherds. To be a pastor is to be both shepherd and theologian—the two roles mutually inform one another and cannot be separated. Pastors care for the people God has gathered to their congregations. Both doctrinal error and relational heresy destroy them and their churches. Doctrinal error can occur in the act of speaking wrongly of God and the biblical witness. Relational error can also occur in the way we relate to and interact with others. Both are caustic, toxic, and mar the church and her ministry. Because associate pastors sit in the pinched middle of their congregations, the responsibility to apply doctrine well in relationships is high; the likelihood that they may be treated poorly is higher because of the web of connections they experience; and the pressure they feel to misuse power or abuse relationships may also be high because of the pressures that come with being in the middle of a congregation.

I think it is therefore incumbent on theological education to refine ministerial students' existing relational competencies or develop relational competencies in the context of a Christian ethic. But I think developing relational competencies will require more than, but not less than, field education and internships. It is not enough to relegate relational skill training merely to "on-the-job-training." If theory and practice are locked in a praxis loop, the seminary setting must provide both classroom and field experience with relational skills.

Further, discernment, if it is a key spiritual practice in relational decision-making in congregations, must also be fostered in seminaries and other educational settings:

> Distinctive to clergy education—in comparison with other forms of professional education—is the necessity of learning to make judgments in reference to some understanding of the presence or leading of God or the dynamics at work in the mystery of human experience in a given situation.
>
> Nurturing capacities for discernment, while engaging students at the edges of their understandings and the limits of their skills, is an especially crucial role in professional education.[2]

I would suggest a four-pronged approach to teaching theologically informed relational competency. First, students need to be

---

2   Foster, Dahill, Golemon, and Tolentino, *Educating Clergy*, 122.

exposed to introductory literature that orients them to organizational literature, congregational dynamics, and relational competency. Second, students should learn how to practice negotiation, discourse, dialogue, and discernment. Third, students should understand themselves, their own anxieties, and how they tend to function in family systems. Fourth, students must observe how complexity and ambiguity work in actual congregations, and reflect on their own responses and actions in that ambiguity.

I suggest that four learning environments be utilized to help ministry students achieve these learning goals. First, basic theological, theoretical, and practical frameworks for relationships should be taught in the classroom. Second, an accompanying skills training class should be included that inculcates the skills for negotiation, discourse, dialogue, and discernment. Third, students should be required to engage in personal spiritual formation with a caring mentor while in school. Fourth, students should observe and practice relational dynamics in their field education.

Traditional Classroom

The traditional classroom could be a recurring half-credit class which meets weekly for fifty-five minutes. Since associate pastors dive into management and leadership literature shortly after beginning ministry out of necessity, seminary should aim to pre-equip them with some advanced reading which grounds them in theory oriented to practice before graduation.

Over the course of ministerial training, I would recommend that seminary students read the following seven resources. These books provide an introduction into organizational pressures, personal spiritual health and healthy relationships, theological integration of organizational literature in a missional church model, and discernment:

1. *Resilient Ministry* by Bob Burns, Tasha Chapman, and Don Guthrie
2. *The Emotionally Healthy Leader* by Peter Scazzero
3. *Congregational Leadership in Anxious Times* by Peter Steinke

4. *Ministry in the Image of God* by David Seamands
5. *Discerning God's Will Together* by Ruth Haley Barton
6. *The Ministry of the Missional Church* by Craig Van Gelder
7. *Leading from the Second Chair* by Michael Bonem and Roger Patterson

Discourse Laboratory

The discourse laboratory is an environment which specializes in teaching the skills of negotiation, discourse, dialogue, and discernment. This specialized class might meet weekly for fifty-five to eighty minutes and would ground students in the specific processes and practices of each form of congregational communication. Essentially, this functions along the same lines as a preaching laboratory, where students can practice in a controlled setting, make mistakes without hurting actual congregations, and experience helpful correction. Discussions would be guided through robust case studies and role playing; students would be required to take positions as key leaders, associate pastors, elders, and senior pastors as they worked through various ambiguous situations in a simulated complex congregation. Students would be required to learn how to facilitate discernment sessions, and would learn key skills such as listening to understand, empathy, and silence.

Spiritual Formation Setting

Since associate pastors describe affirming their pastoral identity as a significant motivation for facilitating their own learning while on the job, seminary students need to realize that their ministries are given them by God, even when some stakeholders in their congregational systems may not affirm them as pastors. The ability to maintain nonanxious presence and self-differentiation is critical to this task. Seminary students should be learning to pay attention to their own anxieties in their current academic and work environments. Who are they likely to triangle into stressful situations and why? If they have a spouse or significant other, what stresses and challenges are present in these relationships that unsettle them?

Spiritual formation grounds students in their relationship with God so that their personalities and gifts are transformed and submitted to God's reign. Spiritual formation requires a capacity to carefully open oneself to a caring guide.

Field Education and Internships

Field education creates opportunities for seminary students to have guided ministerial experience in actual congregations under the watchful eye of pastoral mentors. Often field education provides specific hands-on ministry in preaching, teaching, and discipleship, with deep dives in special zones of ministry such as youth or worship. Seminary students should take the opportunities afforded by extensive field education and internships to see how the pastoral staff navigates the complexities that occur in congregational life. While field education may require other assignments, I would suggest a journal assignment where, on a weekly or semiweekly basis, ministry students keep track of all the anxious interactions they observe or personally experience. Questions they should attempt to answer might be:

1. Who were the participants in the ambiguous moment?
2. What were they anxious about in that moment?
3. What was at stake in the interaction for each person?
4. What did you feel in the interaction?
5. How did a leader point to a helpful resolution either through critical reflection, negotiation, discourse, or discernment?
6. How was the triune God brought into the experience?

At the end of the semester, seminarians should write a short (three-page) essay reflecting on their anxiety or emotional response to ambiguity, how they handled that specific anxiety or emotional response, and how they worked to resolve the ambiguity itself. They should also reflect on their ability to apply negotiation, discourse, or discernment in resolving ambiguity, particularly as they worked to include appropriate stakeholders in any decision and how they sought the Holy Spirit's wisdom and guidance in the ambiguous moment.

Last Word

One of the friends I mentioned in the beginning of this afterword asked me, "Would you ever go back into congregational ministry again?" I answered firmly, "Yes." Associate pastoral ministry is no doubt a challenging vocation. But it is also full of joy, fruitfulness, and life. I enjoy congregational and elder board meetings, training meetings, and planning meetings because I see the value of relationships. Life in the church, the body of Christ, is profoundly and inherently relational, and relationships can be sources of life, joy, and mutual ministry. As Jesus said, "where two or three are gathered in my name, there I am among them" (Matt. 18:20). But many of the skills I needed I learned either on my own or as a part of my PhD studies. No one can ever enter ministry fully prepared for the challenges they will face in their specific congregations. Thanks to on-the-job learning and experience, I am a far more competent theologian, preacher, teacher, and counselor fifteen years after my graduation from seminary than when I began. But just as I had training in preaching and counseling in seminary, so training in managing and relationships would have helped avoid painful mistakes early in my ministry after seminary.

Just as theology, preaching, teaching, and counseling are key elements of pastoral practice, so is learning to manage complex relationships. So, allowing for growth in the future practice of a graduate, let us give advance preparation for those who will share in the ministry of the middle.

BIBLIOGRAPHY

Akinde, Oluwatoyin A. "A Study Comparing the Leadership and Management Characteristics of Associate Church Pastors and Mid-Level Corporate Managers and Leaders: An Analysis Based on Member Feedback." EdD diss., Saint Mary's University of Minnesota, 2012.

Argyris, Chris. *Interpersonal Competence and Organizational Effectiveness*. New York: Richard D. Irwin, 1968.

Argyris, Chris, and Donald A. Schön. *Theory in Practice: Increasing Professional Effectiveness*. San Francisco: Jossey-Bass, 1974.

———. *Organizational Learning II: Theory, Method, and Practice*. Reading, MA: Addison-Wesley Publishing, 1996.

Ashford, Bruce Riley, and Heath A. Thomas. *The Gospel of Our King: Bible, Worldview, and the Mission of Every Christian*. Grand Rapids: Baker Academic, 2019.

Barton, Ruth Haley. *Pursuing God's Will Together: A Discernment Practice for Leadership Groups*. Downers Grove, IL: InterVarsity, 2012.

Bateson, Gregory. *Steps to an Ecology of Mind*. 2nd ed. Chicago: University of Chicago Press, 2000.

Bertalanffy, Ludwig von. *General System Theory: Foundations, Developments, Applications*. New York: George Braziller, 1969.

Block, Peter. *Stewardship: Choosing Service Over Self-Interest*. 2nd ed. San Francisco: Berrett-Koehler, 2013.

Boersma, Stephen Anthony. "Managerial Competencies for Church Administration as Perceived by Seminary Faculties, Church Lay Leaders, and Ministers." PhD diss., Oregon State University, 1988.

Bohm, David. *Wholeness and the Implicate Order*. New York: Routledge, 1980.

———. *On Dialogue*. New York: Routledge, 1996.

Bonem, Mike, and Robert Patterson. *Leading from the Second Chair: Serving Your Church, Fulfilling Your Role, and Realizing Your Dreams*. San Francisco: Jossey-Bass, 2005.

Bosworth, Susan Lovegreen, and Gary A. Kreps. "Structure as Process: Organization and Role." *American Sociological Review* 51, no. 4: 699–716, 1986.

Branson, Mark Lau, and Juan F. Martínez. *Churches, Cultures, and Leadership: A Practical Theology of Congregations and Ethnicities*. Downers Grove, IL: IVP Academic, 2011.

Breshears, Elizabeth M., and Roger D. Volker. *Facilitative Leadership in Social Work Practice*. New York: Springer, 2013.

Brookfield, Stephen D. *Teaching for Critical Thinking: Tools and Techniques to Help Students Question Their Assumptions*. San Francisco: Jossey-Bass, 2012.

Burns, Bob, Tasha D. Chapman, and Donald C. Guthrie. *Resilient Ministry: What Pastors Told Us about Thriving and Surviving*. Downers Grove, IL: InterVarsity Press, 2013.

———. *The Politics of Ministry: Navigating Power Dynamics and Negotiating Interests*. Downers Grove, IL: InterVarsity Press, 2019.

Cervero, Ronald. M., and Arthur. L. Wilson. *Planning Responsibly for Adult Education: A Guide to Negotiating Power and Interests*. San Francisco: Jossey-Bass, 1994.

———. *Working the Planning Table: Negotiating Democratically for Adult, Continuing, and Workplace Education*. San Francisco: John Wiley and Sons, 2006.

Chaleef, Ira. *The Courageous Follower: Standing Up to and for Our Leaders*. 3rd ed. San Francisco: Berrett-Koehler, 2009.

Charry, Ellen T. *By the Renewing of Your Minds: The Pastoral Function of Theology*. New York: Oxford, 1997.

Checkland, Peter. *Systems Thinking, Systems Practice*. Chicester, UK: John Wiley and Sons, 1981.

Chrysostom, St. John. *Six Books on the Priesthood*. Translated by G. Neville. Crestwood, NY: St. Vladimir's Press, 1977.

Cooper, Cary L., Philip J. Dewe, and Michael P. O'Driscoll. *Organizational Stress: A Review ad Critique of Theory, Research, and Applications*. Thousand Oaks, CA: Sage, 2001.

Covey, Stephen R. *The 7 Habits of Highly Effective People: Powerful Lessons in Personal Change*. New York: Simon and Schuster, 1989.

Cranton, Patricia. *Understanding and Promoting Transformative Learning: A Guide for Educators of Adults*. 2nd ed. San Francisco: Jossey-Bass, 2006.

Danyluk, Bill Roy. "The Process of Hiring Associate Pastoral Staff in Congregationally Governed Churches with a Worship Attendance of under 300." DMin diss., Trinity Evangelical Divinity School, 2005.

Dean, Kenda Creasy. *Practicing Passion: Youth and the Quest for a Passionate Church*. Grand Rapids: Eerdmans, 2004.

DeVries, Mark. *Sustainable Youth Ministry: Why Most Youth Ministry Doesn't Last and What Your Church Can Do about It*. Downers Grove, IL: InterVarsity Press, 2008.

Drane, John. *The McDonaldization of the Church: Consumer Culture and the Church's Future*. Macon, GA: Smyth & Helwys, 2000.

Drucker, Peter F. *Managing the Nonprofit Organization: Principles and Practice*. San Francisco, CA: Harper Business, 2005.

Drucker, Peter F., with Joseph A. Maciariello. *Management*. Rev. ed. San Francisco: Harper Business, 2008.

Ellinger, Andrea D. "Antecedents and Consequences of Coaching Behavior." *Performance Improvement Quarterly* 16, no. 1: 5–28, 2003.

Ellinger, Andrea D., and Robert P. Bostrom. "Managerial Coaching Behaviors in Learning Organizations." *The Journal of Management Development* 18, no. 9: 752–771, 1999.

_____. "An Examination of Managers' Beliefs about Their Roles and Facilitators of Learning." *Management Learning* 33, no. 2: 147–179, 2002.

Ellinger, Andrea A. D., Karen E. Watkins, and Robert P. Bostrom. "Managers as Facilitators of Learning in Learning Organizations." *Human Resources Development Quarterly* 10, no. 2: 105–125, 1999.

Elmer, Muriel I., and Duane H. Elmer. *The Learning Cycle: Insights for Faithful Teaching from Neuroscience and the Social Sciences.* Downers Grove, IL: IVP Academic, 2020.

Esa, Donald R. "Issues in Ministry Effectiveness for the Associate Pastor." DMin diss., Fuller Theological Seminary, 1996.

Even, Linda D. "Applying Systems Theory to the Entry of the Associate Pastor into a New Congregational System as Model and Means for Lay Employment." DMin diss., Drew University, 2002.

Faucett, John M., Robert F. Corwyn, and Tom H. Poling. "Clergy Role Stress: Interactive Effects of Role Ambiguity and Role Conflict on Intrinsic Job Satisfaction." *Pastoral Psychology* 62, no. 3: 291–304, 2013.

Fisher, Roger, William Ury, and Bruce Patton. *Getting to Yes: Negotiating Agreement without Giving In.* 2nd ed. New York: Penguin, 1991.

Forester, John. *Planning in the Face of Power.* Berkeley and Los Angeles: University of California Press, 1989.

———. "Learning from Practice in the Face of Conflict and Integrating Technical Expertise with Participatory Planning: Critical Commentaries on the Practice of Planner-Architect Laurence Sherman." *Planning Theory and Practice* 12, no. 2: 287–310, 2011.

Foster, Charles, Lisa E. Dahill, Lawrence A. Golemon, and Barbara Wang Tolentino. *Educating Clergy: Teaching Practices and Pastoral Imagination.* San Francisco: Jossey-Bass, 2006.

French, Robert, and John Bazalgette. "From 'Learning Organization' to 'Teaching-Learning Organization'?" *Management Learning* 27, no. 1: 113–128, 1996.

Friedman, Edwin H. *Generation to Generation: Family Process in Church and Synagogue.* New York: Guilford Press, 1985.

Fryer, Mick. "Facilitative Leadership: Drawing on Jurgen Habermas' Model of Ideal Speech to Propose a Less Impositional Way to Lead." *Organization* 19, no. 1: 25–43, 2011.

Gilbreath, Sammy Lee. "An Administrative Manual for the Associate Pastor-Administrator of the First Baptist Church, Huntsville, Alabama." DMin diss., Drew University, 1984.

Goheen, Michael, and Craig Bartholomew. *Living at the Crossroads: An Introduction to Christian Worldview.* Grand Rapids: Baker Academic, 2008.

Greasley, Stephen, and Gerry Stoker. "Mayors and Urban Governance: Developing a Facilitative Leadership Style." *Public Administration Review* 68, no. 4: 722–730, 2008.

Greenleaf, Robert K. *Servant Leadership: A Journey into the Nature of Legitimate Power and Greatness.* 25th Anniversary ed. New York: Paulist Press, 2002.

St. Gregory the Great. *The Book of Pastoral Rule.* Translated by G. A. Demacopoulos. Crestwood, NY: St. Vladimir's Press, 2007.

Griffin, Gordon Everett. "Vision Building as a Second Chair Leader for a Large Congregation." DMin diss., Asbury Seminary, 2009.

Guastello, Stephen J. "Facilitative Style, Individual Innovation, and Emergent Leadership in Problem Solving Groups." *The Journal of Creative Behavior* 29, no. 4: 225–239, 1995.

Guder, Daniel L., ed. *Missional Church: A Vision for the Sending Church in North America.* Grand Rapids: Eerdmans, 1998.

Guthrie, Donald. C. "Facilitated Agency: A Promising Pedagogy." *Christian Educational Journal* 12, no. 1: 162–177, 2015.

Hargrove, Robert. 1995. *Masterful Coaching: Extraordinary Results by Impacting People and the Way They Think and Work Together.* San Francisco: Jossey-Bass, 1995.

Haskins, Bruce Franklin. "An Examination of the Role and Function of the Associate Pastor in the United Methodist Church." PhD diss., Howard University, 1991.

Hawkins, Martin E. "An Evaluation of Selected Dallas Theological Seminary Alumni of Assistant and Associate Pastor in the Local Church." DMin diss., Dallas Theological Seminary, 2000.

Hawkins, Martin E., with Kelli Sallman. *The Associate Pastor: Second Chair, Not Second Best.* Nashville: Broadman and Hollman, 2005.

Hawkins, Peter. "The Spiritual Dimension of the Learning Organisation." *Management Education and Development* 22, no. 3: 172–187, 1991.

Heifetz, Ronald A., Alexander Grashow, and Martin Linsky. *The Practice of Adaptive Leadership: Tools and Tactics for Changing Your Organization and the World*. Boston: Harvard Business Review Press, 2009.

Herrington, Jim, R. Robert Creech, and Trisha Taylor. *The Leader's Journey: Accepting the Call to Personal and Congregational Transformation*. San Francisco: Jossey-Bass, 2003.

Hiestand, Gerald, and Todd A. Wilson. *The Pastor Theologian: Resurrecting an Ancient Vision*. Grand Rapids: Zondervan, 2015.

Hilbert, Robert A. "Toward an Improved Understanding of 'Role.'" *Theory and Society* 10, no. 2: 207–226, 1981.

Hollander, Edwin P. *Leadership Dynamics: A Practical Guide to Effective Relationships*. New York: Free Press, 1978.

Isaacs, William. *Dialogue and the Art of Thinking Together*. New York, New York: Currency, 199.

Jackson, Michael C. *Systems Thinking: Creating Holism for Managers*. Chicester, UK: John Wiley and Sons, 2003.

Johnson, Dean D. "Preparing an Associate Pastor to Become a Senior Pastor." DMin diss., Trinity Evangelical Divinity School, 2003.

Kahn, Robert L., D. M. Wolfe, Robert P. Quinn, Diedrick Snoek, and Robert A. Rosenthal. *Organizational Stress: Studies in Role Conflict and Ambiguity*. New York: John Wiley and Sons, 1964.

Katz, Daniel, and Robert L. Kahn. *The Social Psychology of Organizations*. 2nd ed. New York: John Wiley and Sons, 1978.

Kegan, Robert. "What 'Forms' Transform? A Constructive Developmental Approach to Transformative Learning." *Learning as Transformation: Critical Perspectives on a Theory in Progress*, edited by Jack Mezirow. San Francisco: Jossey-Bass, 2000.

Kelley, Robert. *The Power of Followership: How to Create Leaders People Want to Follow and Followers Who Lead Themselves*. New York: Currency, 1992.

Kemery, Edward R. "Clergy Role Stress and Satisfaction: Role Ambiguity Isn't Always Bad." *Pastoral Psychology* 54, no. 6: 561–570, 2006.

Kerr, Michael E., and Murray Bowen. *Family Evaluation*. New York: W. W. Norton and Sons, 1988.

Kim, Daniel H. "The Link between Individual and Organizational Learning." *Sloan Management Review* 35, no. 1: 37–50, 1993.

Kim, Daniel H., and Peter Senge. "Putting Systems into Practice." *System Dynamics Review* 10, nos. 2–3: 277–290, 1994.

Knowles, Malcolm S., Edward L. Holton III, and Richard A. Swanson. *The Adult Learner: The Definitive Classic in Adult and Human Resource Development.* 7th ed. New York: Routledge, 2012.

Kraft, Ralph Wayne. *A Reason to Hope: A Synthesis of Teilhard de Chardin's Vision and Systems Thinking.* Seaside, CA: Intersystems Publications, 1983.

Kraut, Allen. I., Patricia R. Pedigo, D. Douglas McKenna, and Marvin D. Dunette. "The Role of the Manager: What's Really Important in Different Management Jobs." *Academy of Management Executive*: 19, no. 4: 122–129, 1989.

Kolb, David. *Experiential Learning: Experience as the Source of Learning and Development.* Upper Saddle River, NJ: Prentice Hall, 1983.

Laniak, Timothy S. *Shepherds after My Own Heart: Pastoral Traditions and Leadership in the Bible.* Downers Grove, IL: InterVarsity, 2006.

Li, Andrew and Jessica Bagger. "Role Ambiguity and Self-Efficacy: The Moderating Effects of Goal Orientation and Procedural Justice." *Journal of Vocational Behavior*: 73, no. 3: 368–375, 2008.

Linton, Ralph. *The Study of Man.* New York: Appleton-Century Crofts, 1936.

Livermore, David A. *Cultural Intelligence: Improving Your CQ to Engage Our Multicultural World.* Grand Rapids: Baker Academic, 2009.

MacIntyre, Alasdair. *After Virtue: A Study in Moral Theory.* 3rd ed. Notre Dame, IN: University of Notre Dame Press, 2007.

Mackenzie, R. A. "The Management Process in 3D." *Harvard Business Review* 47, no. 6: 80–82, 1969.

Marshall, Collin, and Tony Payne. *The Trellis and the Vine: The Ministry Mind-Shift That Changes Everything.* Kingsford, Australia: Matthias Media, 2009; Kindle edition.

McKnight, Scot. *A Community Called Atonement.* Nashville: Abingdon Press, 2007.

Merriam, Sharon B., and Elizabeth J. Tisdell. *Qualitative Research: A Guide to Design and Implementation.* 4th ed. San Francisco: Jossey-Bass, 2015.

Merriema, Sharon B., and Laura L. Bierema. *Adult Learning: Linking Theory and Practice.* San Francisco: Jossey-Bass, 2014.

Merton, Robert K. "The Role Set: Problems in Sociological Theory." *The British Journal of Sociology* 8, no. 2: 106–120, 1957.

Mezirow, Jack. "Learning to Think Like and Adult: Core Concepts of Transformation Theory." In *Learning as Transformation: Critical Perspectives on a Theory in Progress*, edited by Jack Mezirow. San Francisco: Jossey-Bass, 2000.

Mintzberg, Henry. "The Manager's Job: Folklore and Fact." *Harvard Business Review* 53, no. 4: 49–61, 1975.

Mitchell, Kenneth R. *Multiple Staff Ministries.* Philadelphia: Westminster Press, 1988.

Molina, Carlos, and Jamie L. Callahan. "Fostering Organizational Performance: The Role of Learning and Intrapreneurship." *Journal of European Industrial Training* 30, no. 5: 388–400, 2009.

Moore, Thomas L. "Facilitative Leadership: One Approach to Empowering Staff and Stakeholders." *Library Trends* 53, no. 1: 230–237, 2004.

Ngo, Hang-yue, Sharon Foley, and Raymond Loi. "Work Role Stressors and Turnover Intentions: A Study of Professional Clergy in Hong Kong." *International Journal of Human Resource Management* 16, no. 11: 2133–2146, 2005.

Nonaka, Ikujiro. "Toward Middle-Up-Down Management: Accelerating Information Creation." *Sloan Management Review* 29, no. 3: 9–18, 1988.

———. "A Dynamic Theory of Organizational Knowledge Creation." *Organization Science* 5, no. 1: 14–37, 1994.

Nonaka, Ikujiro and Georg Von Krough. "Tacit Knowledge and Knowledge Conversion: Controversy and Advancement in Organizational Knowledge Creation Theory." *Organization Science* 20, no. 3: 635–652, 2009.

Nouwen, Henri J. M. *In the Name of Jesus: Reflections on Christian Leadership*. New York: Crossroad Books, 1989.

Oden, Thomas. C. *Pastoral Theology: Essentials of Ministry*. San Francisco: HarperOne, 1983.

Oshry, Barry. *In the Middle*. Boston: Power and Systems, 1994.

Overman, Julie Kay. "Associate Pastor as Collaborator: Expanding Women's Ministry for Fulfillment and Stability." DMin diss., United Theological Seminary, 2012.

Palmer, Parker J. *To Know as We Are Known: Education as Spiritual Journey*. San Francisco: HarperOne, 1993.

Parrett, Gary A., and S. Steve Kang. *Teaching the Faith, Forming the Faithful: A Biblical Vision for Education in the Church*. Downers Grove, IL: IVP Academic, 2009.

Patterson, Roger. "A Theological Foundation and Workshop for Subordinate Leaders in the Local Church." DMin diss., Southwestern Baptist Theological Seminary, 2006.

_____. *Theology of the Second Chair: A Theological Foundation for the Subordinate Leader of the Local Church*. Lulu.com, 2009.

Pazmiño, Robert W. *Foundational Issues in Christian Education*. 2nd ed. Grand Rapids: Baker, 1997.

Prickard, Stephen. *Theological Foundations for Collaborative Ministry*. Farnham, UK: Ashgate, 2009.

Radcliffe, Robert J. *The Effective Ministry as an Associate Pastor: Making Beautiful Music as a Ministry Team*. Grand Rapids: Kregel, 1998.

Rees, Erik. S.*H.A.P.E: Finding and Fulfilling Your Unique Purpose for Life*. Grand Rapids: Zondervan, 2006.

Reeves, Michael. *Delighting in the Trinity: An Introduction to the Christian Faith*. Downers Grove, IL: InterVarsity Press, 2012.

Ritzer, George. *The McDonaldization of Society*. 20th Anniversary ed. Thousand Oaks, CA: Sage, 2012.

Rizzo, John R., Robert J. House, and Sidney I. Lirtzman. "Role Conflict and Ambiguity in Complex Organizations." *Administrative Science Quarterly* 15, no. 2: 150–63, 1970.

Rodin, R. Scott. *The Steward Leader: Transforming People, Organizations, and Communities.* Downers Grove, IL: IVP Academic, 2010.

Root, Andrew. *The Pastor in a Secular Age: Ministry to People Who No Longer Need a God.* Grand Rapids: Baker Academic, 2019.

Rudnick, Alan. *The Work of the Associate Pastor.* Valley Forge, PA: Judson Press, 2012.

Sam, Francis Kawme. "The Formation, Mentoring, and Socialization of the Associate Pastor into the Pastorate in the Roman Catholic Church." EdD diss., Fordham University, 1995.

Scazzero, Peter. *The Emotionally Healthy Leader: How Transforming Your Inner Life Will Deeply Transform Your Church, Team, and the World.* Grand Rapids: Zondervan, 2015.

Scharmer, C. Otto. *Theory U: Leading from the Future as It Emerges.* 2nd ed. San Francisco: Berrett-Koehler, 2016.

Scharmer, C. Otto, and Katrin Kaufer. *Leading from the Emerging Future: From Ego System to Eco-System Economies.* San Francisco: Berrett-Koehler, 2013.

Schein, Edgar H. *Organizational Culture and Leadership.* 4th ed. Hoboken, NJ: John Wiley and Sons, 2010.

Schwarz, Christian. *Paradigm Shift in the Church.* Carol Stream, IL: ChurchSmart Resources, 1999.

Schwarz, Roger M. *The Skilled Facilitator: A Comprehensive Resource for Consultants, Facilitators, Managers, Trainees, and Coaches.* 2nd edition. San Francisco: Jossey-Bass, 2016.

Seamands, Stephen. *Ministry in the Image of God: The Trinitarian Shape of Christian Service.* Downers Grove, IL, 2005.

Senge, Peter. *The Fifth Disciple: The Art and Practice of the Learning Organization.* Rev. ed. New York: Currency, 2006.

Senge, Peter, C. Otto Scharmer, Joseph Jaworski, and Betty S. Flowers. *Presence: Human Purpose and the Field of the Future.* Cambridge, MA: SoL, 2004.

Slater, Stanley F., and John C. Narver. "Market Orientation and Organizational Learning." *Journal of Marketing* 59, no. 3: 63–74, 1995.

Smith, C. Christopher, and John Pattison. *Slow Church: Cultivating Community in the Patient Way of Jesus.* Downers Grove, IL: InterVarsity, 2014.

Smith, M. J. "Playing Second Fiddle on One String: The Role of the Associate Pastor." DMin diss., Grace Theological Seminary, 2007.

Snyder, Howard A. *The Community of the King.* Rev. ed. Downers Grove, IL: IVP Academic, 2004.

Song, Ji Hong, and Thomas J. Chermack. "A Theoretical Approach to the Organizational Knowledge Formation Process: Integrating the Concepts of Individual Learning and Learning Organization Culture." *Human Resource Development Review* 7, no. 4: 424–442, 2008.

Steinke, Peter L. *Congregational Leadership in Anxious Times: Being Calm and Courageous No Matter What.* Lanham, MD: Rowman and Littlefield, 2006.

Stout, John K., and Jody L. Posner. "Stress, Role Ambiguity, and Role Conflict." *Psychological Report* 55: 747–753, 1984.

Svara, James H., ed. *Facilitative Leadership in Local Government: Lessons from Successful Mayors and Chairpersons.* San Francisco: Jossey-Bass, 1994.

Swieringa, Joop, and Andre Wierdsma. *Becoming a Learning Organization: Beyond the Learning Curve.* Wokingham, UK: Addison Wesley, 1992.

Tidball, Derek. *Skilful Shepherds: Explorations in Pastoral Theology.* Leicester, Great Britain: Apollos, 1997.

Töremen, Fatih. "A Study of Facilitative Leadership Behavior and Its Role in the Success of Schools." *International Journal of Educational Reform* 13, no. 3: 295–306, 2004.

Tsui, Anne S., Susan J. Ashford, Lynda St. Clair, and Katherine R. Xin. "Dealing with Discrepant Expectations: Response Strategies and Managerial Effectiveness." *Academy of Management Journal*: 36, no. 6: 1515–43, 1995.

Turner, Ralph H. "Strategy for Developing an Integrated Role Theory." *Humboldt Journal of Social Relations* 7, no. 1: 123–39, 1979.

Uhl-Bien, Mary, Ronald E. Riggio, Kevin B. Lowe, and Melissa K. Carsten. "Followership Theory: A Review and Research Agenda." *Leadership Quarterly* 25, no. 1: 83–104, 2014.

Vanhoozer, Kevin J., and Owen Strachan. *The Pastor as Public Theologian: Reclaiming a Lost Vision.* Grand Rapids: Baker, 2015.

Van Gelder, Craig. *The Ministry of the Missional Church: A Community Led by the Spirit.* Grand Rapids: Baker, 2007.

Van Sell, Mary, Arthur P. Brief, and Randall S. Schuler. "Role Conflict and Role Ambiguity: Integration of the Literature and Directions for Future Research." *Human Relations* 34, no. 1: 43–71, 1981.

Volf, Miroslav, and Matthew Croasmun. *For the Life of the World: Theology That Makes a Difference.* Grand Rapids: Brazos Press, 2019.

Waltke, Bruce, K., with Kathi J. Fredricks. *Genesis: A Commentary.* Grand Rapids: Zondervan, 2001.

Walton, John H. *Ancient Near Eastern Thought and the Old Testament: Introducing the Conceptual World of the Hebrew Bible.* Grand Rapids: Baker Academic, 2006.

_____. *The Lost World of Genesis One: Ancient Cosmology and the Origins Debate.* Downers Grove, IL: IVP Academic, 2009.

Ward, Pete. *Introducing Practical Theology: Mission, Ministry, and the Life of the Church.* Grand Rapids: Baker Academic, 2017.

Watson, J. B., and Walter H. Scalen, Jr. "'Dining with the Devil': The Unique Secularization of American Evangelical Churches." *International Social Science Review* 83, nos. 3–4: 171–80, 2008.

Weick, Karl E. *Sensemaking in Organizations.* Thousand Oaks, CA: Sage, 1995.

Wenger, Etienne. *Communities of Practice: Learning, Meaning, and Identity.* Cambridge, UK: Cambridge University Press, 1998.

Wenham, Gordon J. *Genesis 1–15.* World Biblical Commentary. Waco, TX: Nelson Reference and Electronic, 1987.

Westing, Harold J. *Church Staff Handbook: How to Build an Effective Ministry Team.* 2nd ed. Grand Rapids: Kregel, 1997.

Willimon, William H. *Pastor: The Theology and Practice of Ordained Ministry.* Nashville: Abingdon, 2002.

Wilson, Kent R. *Steward Leadership in the Nonprofit Organization.* Downers Grove, IL: InterVarsity, 2016.

Woodruff, Timothy Rowland. "Executive Pastor's Perception of Leadership and Management Competencies Needed for Local Church Administration." EdD diss., The Southern Baptist Theological Seminary, 2004.

Wright, Christopher J. H. *The Mission of God's People: A Biblical Theology of the Church's Mission.* Grand Rapids: Zondervan, 2010.

Younger, K. Lawson. *Judges, Ruth.* Grand Rapids: Zondervan, 2002.